THE WISDOM OF N

The Wisdom of
NAZARETH

Stories of Catholic Family Life

Selected and Edited by
Sr Crucis Beards FMDM and Anna Schafer
Foreword by Lord Alton
Introduction by Michael O'Brien

FAMILY PUBLICATIONS • OXFORD
MARYVALE INSTITUTE

published by

Family Publications
6A King St, Oxford, OX2 6DF, UK
www.familypublications.co.uk

and

Centre for Marriage and Family at The Maryvale Institute
Maryvale House,
Old Oscott Hill, Birmingham, B44 9AG, UK
www.maryvale.ac.uk

Cover picture *The Presentation* by Michael O'Brien
Line drawings by Roseanne Sharpe

printed in England through
ss media limited

Contents

Motherhood

Fatherhood

Marriage

Family Life

To every Catholic family

Acknowledgments

This book would not be possible without the numerous families and family members whose stories are told in these pages. To them we owe the greatest debt of thanks. These stories, in turn, would not have been made available were it not for the generous and untiring work of so many who were associated with the *Nazareth Journal* and the Nazareth Family Apostolate. We have tried to reach the authors of the pieces which appear in this book. Where we have not managed to do so, we would ask them to contact the publisher at the Centre for Marriage and Family at The Maryvale Institute, Old Oscott Hill, Birmingham, B44 9AG, England.

Our thanks go to Michael O'Brien, novelist, artist and an outstanding champion in his dedication to the fostering of Catholic culture and family life, for honouring us with an introduction to this book. We are also most grateful to Professor Lord David Alton of Liverpool who has written the Foreword. It is with great delight that we thank Miss Roseanne Sharpe of the Bethlehem Community, Bathgate, North Dakota, USA for contributing exquisite line drawings to this text. We are especially pleased that this collection of family stories has been thus illustrated by a member of a community so committed to authentic family life.

We must also record special thanks to Miss Mary Schafer who has patiently and expertly prepared this text for publication; to Joseph Smiles, Projects Director of the Centre for Marriage and Family at The Maryvale Institute, and Petroc Willey, Deputy Director of The Maryvale Institute, who have provided much of the energy behind this project; and to the wider families of The Maryvale Institute and Family Publications who have sponsored the appearance of this work.

Sr Crucis Beards
Anna Schafer

Feast of the Holy Family, 2007

Foreword

It gives me great happiness to endorse this first publication of the Centre for Marriage and Family at The Maryvale Institute imprint of Family Publications. The personal stories in this volume have been drawn from a series produced some years ago in the *Nazareth Journal*, a wonderful family journal originally edited by Michael O'Brien. Michael will be well-known to many of us – as an artist, a novelist and a courageous exponent of Catholic teaching on the family. I am very glad that he has encouraged the re-publication of these stories and has provided a stimulating introduction to the book.

The stories have come to us from 'across the water' – mainly from Canada – but they have a perennial value and speak beautifully of so many family situations. It is my hope, and my belief, that readers in the British Isles and beyond will find in this collection great sources of encouragement as they read about ordinary families coping with difficulties and challenges in family life, often with humour and always with a profound sense of faith.

As we all know, both marriage and the family are often seen to be marginalised. It is therefore greatly to be welcomed that the internationally-renowned Maryvale Institute has now established its Centre for Marriage and Family and has undertaken, in association with Family Publications, the setting up of this imprint for publishing material aimed at supporting marriage and family life. This first publication of the Centre, *The Wisdom of Nazareth: Stories of Catholic Family Life*, vividly demonstrates the deeply pro-life nature of the Church's teaching through these personal testimonies.

In his Angelus address on 30 December 2007, on the Feast of the Holy Family, the Holy Father, Pope Benedict XVI, urged Christian families to 'experience the loving presence of the Lord in their lives by drawing inspiration from Christ's love for mankind, to bear witness before the world of the beauty of human love, of marriage and of the family'. Through this publication, and through the work of the Centre in general, I hope and pray that all of us will indeed become ever more deeply convinced of the beauty of human love, marriage and the family.

Professor David Alton, Lord Alton of Liverpool

Introduction

It is a great pleasure for me, indeed a great joy, to introduce this anthology of selected articles from *Nazareth Journal*. For those readers unfamiliar with its origins, the journal arose as one of several works of a Catholic family apostolate that thrived in Canada during the 1980s and 1990s. Its retreat centre in Combermere, Ontario, hosted thousands of families during its lifetime, and had as its particular focus the teachings of Pope John Paul II on marriage and the family. At that time, human sexuality throughout the West had become increasingly infected by dissident moral theology combined with the neglect of authentic pastoral formation, notably in some particular churches of the affluent nations. Yet the outpouring of extraordinary teaching from the Magisterium, through its documents on the family and the encyclicals of her popes, had never been so rich, so inspired, and now it was opening up a vast horizon for married couples, giving them unprecedented resources for their vocation – a vocation that is simultaneously a most fragile and powerful thing, the 'domestic Church', and the foundation of civilization itself. One thinks of the encyclicals *Humanae Vitae* and *Familiaris Consortio*, of John Paul II's Theology of the Body and of numerous other documents that informed us and encouraged us, that deepened our understanding of the greatness of our vocation, helping us to see in all the apparent weaknesses of married life the 'glorious ordinary' of Nazareth. In a word, a path to holiness, and to eternal fruitfulness.

As the founders of Nazareth Family Apostolate sought to redress the lamentable gap between formation and practice, they saw that Catholic families drew much strength from each other as they told their personal stories of hopes and struggles, successes and failures. Building upon this phenomenon, a family magazine swiftly developed into a quarterly magazine that just grew and grew. During the seven years I was the editor of *Nazareth Journal*,

I was astonished at how hungrily and gratefully it was received by thousands of families throughout the world. This underlined for me the practically universal need for solid and lively communication – an integration of orthodox teachings with the ways we can incarnate them in our families. The stories themselves, written from the front lines, sometimes on hill tops and sometimes in fox holes, bridged the gap.

In this anthology you will find many such stories, written by men and women who have sought to live the fullness of our Catholic faith, often against great odds, with courage and with love. There is a self-honesty here, a constant humility heard between the lines, which points to the widespread awareness that we have been to some extent deprived of our sacramental 'birthright', if you will, and that nothing less than Truth can heal and restore us. 'The Truth spoken in Love' was the constant guidepost for our writers and editorial choices. Thus, the authors you will meet through these pages are people who, like you, know that much is at stake, primarily the spiritual health of our children and the strengthening of our marriages. Moreover, that we live in what John Paul II called a 'culture of death' has escaped no one's notice, for anyone who strives for openness to life, to live according to Natural Law and illumined by sanctifying grace, cannot fail to enter a world of struggle. It is also, it should be noted, a world of great and unexpected joys – joys that are united to the path of sacrifice and trust exemplified by the Holy Family of Nazareth. In short, the 'ordinary' life of faithful Catholic marriage and family is one that leads to the Cross – and thus, it is also one of resurrection.

If the dimension of resurrection has been too often neglected in reflections on the state of the family in the modern age, in this collection can be found the proper integration. Too often, a conscious or subconscious rationalism has infected the thinking of contemporary man, even men of good will, and one could go so far as to say many a churchman as well. In their assessments of what is 'reasonable' and possible for marriage in our times they minimalised, or dismissed altogether, the factors of grace and the transforming power of sacrificial love.

The authors of the articles included in this collection learned to see how crippling such an attitude really is and turned instead to Christ. Invoking his aid, nourished by the universal Church, little by little they advanced in the 'Great School of the Soul' that is married life and family. For none of them was it easy. In taking their first tentative steps of trust, they grew stronger, wiser, and then their strides became longer and surer. Trust grew, and with it love grew, and in the process they bore fruit that will last.

Michael D. O'Brien
Combermere, Ontario, Canada

Motherhood

One

My Master's Degree

by Mariette Ulrich

With the passing of another May passes also the annual spring convocation at my alma mater, the University of Saskatchewan. I note it now with only fleeting interest, but at one time this stately event could not take place without my feeling a sense of loss and regret. Eight years ago, I was accepted into graduate studies at the university, but never went and consequently did not earn an MA in English Literature, as I had planned. Somewhat by default, I stayed home and took up full-time mothering, homemaking and, most recently, home-schooling. In the eyes of the world I am 'just' a housewife. In the eyes of the Lord, however, I am infinitely more, and it is only through his grace that I have come to truly appreciate having chosen the better part.

I received my bachelor's degree as a newly-wed living in Swift Current, Saskatchewan, where my husband Dan was working on a short-term contract. I heartily disliked our new town – it had no symphony orchestra – and wanted to return to Saskatoon. I had no idea what to do with my life – it hadn't occurred to me to ask God – so I decided to try post-graduate studies. Dan encouraged my decision, as his job was temporary and we anticipated a move at some point anyway. I applied to college in the fall and looked for a job to while away the next ten months. I intended to work until the following August, then move back to Saskatoon to resume my academic career. Dan would follow when his contract expired.

I found a job, and our plan hummed smoothly along until one

morning in January, when we observed with consternation that I was experiencing a rather long run of high temperatures. Dan and I had been 'using' NFP – not living it – and were not particularly open to the idea of having a child just then. When the pregnancy was confirmed, we felt anxious and overwhelmed. Over the next few weeks, Dan quickly adjusted to the notion of impending parenthood, but I lapsed into depression as severe nausea forced me to spend several seeks in bed, too ill to do anything but stare at the ceiling and bemoan my situation.

My relationship with God had long been in a downward spiral, mostly because of a non-existent prayer life, stubbornly-held vestiges of feminism and watery theology I'd absorbed at university. This pregnancy didn't improve my spiritual life: I blamed God for the whole predicament – somehow forgetting certain biological facts – and felt as though my life had taken a decisive turn for the worse.

My spirits rallied when the nausea subsided and soon plans were underway, not only for labour, delivery and purchases of baby things but also for my 'life after baby', which naturally included grad school and a real job. My acceptance into the MA programme was valid for two years, so I planned to take one year off and stay home with the baby, breast feeding for eight or nine months. Then, when baby turned one – and didn't need me anymore – I would hand her off to a sitter, and begin work on my master's degree.

Midway through my second trimester, the university awarded me a generous scholarship. I was stunned, especially when I realised that in order to use the funds, I had to begin my program of study in the upcoming fall session, just days after the baby was due. Although my decision had already been made, it was with a heavy heart that I relinquished the money, wondering, for the hundredth time, what 'might have been' had I not become pregnant. My disappointment only strengthened my resolve to return to school the following year – scholarship or no scholarship.

Summer finally neared its end, and early in the morning of September 3, I began eighteen hours of difficult labour. During the transition stage, I remember thinking, 'If I can make it through this alive, getting my master's degree ought to be a snap!' And then our baby was born.

Giving birth was an awe-inspiring experience, and beholding that tiny perfect infant brought me as close to God as I had been for many years. To my great surprise, I fell in love with little Christine immediately, as up to this point I'd considered myself as un-maternal as a woman could be – my sociology classes had convinced me that the maternal instinct was merely a construction of patriarchy. I couldn't comprehend the emotions that filled my heart as I watched her funny facial expressions, stroked her soft skin, felt her heartbeat and pondered the miracle of human life.

With awe soon giving way to sleepless nights, Dan and I joined all new parents in the delights and frustrations, fumbles and little triumphs, of life with a new baby. Since Christine cried much of the night, and slept or nursed most of the day, I saw very little of Dan. Our baby wanted to be held by Mom all the time, and he slept in the spare room when not cooking, cleaning or washing diapers. I enjoyed long-distance support from our large extended family, but since I knew few people in Swift Current, I experienced many lonely days in those early months. My sense of isolation eased somewhat when I met other mothers through a breast feeding support group, but having friends was not enough to content me.

The challenges of my daily life were a far cry from the bustling and stimulating world of university. Housework, cooking and baby-care accorded me little satisfaction, no intellectual stimulation, no pay, no worldly status. I disliked being referred to as a housewife and felt depressed at the idea of spending a lifetime at home. I loved Christine very much and enjoyed being with her, but deep down believed I needed more than motherhood and homemaking to be 'fulfilled'.

An extension of Dan's work contract some months later meant we would not be moving back to Saskatoon as planned. This did not sit well with me; I obstinately wanted to return to school and earn my master's degree, without even knowing what, if any, useful application it would have for our family's life.

Dan began to question the practicality of my scheme, bringing up minor details like childcare and how we would survive financially if he couldn't find a job. I became angry and defensive. I accused him of being basely utilitarian and insisted that education for its own sake was a noble thing – easy for me to say in my well-fed and sheltered state. I used tired old 'sexism' to defend my cause, insisting with an injured air that my aspirations had no value in his eyes simply because I was a woman. What bothered me most of all, and pride and stubbornness kept me from admitting, was that he was absolutely right in every regard.

I wanted that degree, if for no other reason than to have the extra letters behind my name. In some vague way, I thought they would make me a better person, or at least a more important one, although I knew deep down that such things mean nothing to God. I vacillated between resentment, self-pity and guilt. I knew my attitude displeased God, but ultimately didn't care; pleasing myself was my main object. Since I could not have my heart's desire, I suffered, and my family suffered with me.

When Christine was eight months old, I once again became unexpectedly pregnant and unpredictably disconsolate. I panicked about the spacing, envisioning myself nine months hence, with a toddler and a newborn – how would I ever manage? In my wounded pride, I dreaded the comments from others, certain to be elicited by our news – most of the people I knew never made 'mistakes', and averaged a much more respectable span between children. Here I was, an educated woman, about to do double diaper duty, my mind wasting away, my life on hold, no hope in sight. I felt I could not cope with what lay ahead, and in my despondency I asked God to let the cup pass from me.

'You should be careful what you pray for lest it be granted to you'; I learned the lesson of that saying in a very bitter way. Eleven weeks into the pregnancy I began spotting. Two days later I suffered a miscarriage in the hospital. I'd naively thought my grief would be lessened because I had not 'wanted' the baby, but my sorrow was only intensified by deep remorse. I knew that God must have ordained our baby's life and death to some purpose, perhaps in part to bring me closer to him and enable me to truly value the gift of life. Whatever his reasons, it was a hard lesson and a high price for the jolt out of my self-centredness. I have since experienced God's healing and forgiveness, but knowing that the empty space in our family will never be filled leaves a lingering sadness.

Nearly two years passed. Dan's contract finally seemed to be coming to a close. We made tentative plans to return to Saskatoon, and I began to think about reapplying to the MA programme at the university. In our uncertain situation, we deemed it necessary to put family-expansion on hold, and I foolishly said aloud to a friend, 'Of course, we're not going to have any more children until I get my degree'.

God must have someone employed full-time to follow up on silly definitive statements we humans like to make, just to remind us who is in charge. Within two weeks of my uttering those words, Dan's contract was – coincidentally – renewed for a few more years, and so was mine. That is to say, I found myself pregnant once more. Again the conception had been more or less on God's terms, but we were completely receptive, and since Dan's job had been extended, I didn't mind postponing grad school yet again.

Towards the end of this pregnancy, a fellow parishioner invited me to join a mothers' 'faith-sharing' group. We met one afternoon each week to watch and discuss the Nazareth Apostolate's *Restoring Our Family to Christ* video series. During the first session, I felt somewhat irritated when the host suggested that I 'accept my vocation' and be happy in my role as 'heart of the home'. I had bigger and better plans. But by the end of that same session, I was hooked. Something about the session, more specifically, something about the people appearing in it, strongly appealed to me. These families seemed peace-filled and joyful. Seeing them caused my soul to ache with an intense emptiness. They possessed something that I wanted desperately, even more desperately than a master's degree. Though I did not realise it at the time, I longed to know

Jesus again, and spiritually, I wanted to come home.

As the weeks went on, I noted that each segment of the series began with a quotation from an intriguing work called *Familiaris Consortio*. What was it? If it was so significant, why hadn't I ever heard of it before? At university I had been led to believe, by all too many priests, nuns and 'Catholic' professors, that the Pope was everything from ignorant to backward to malicious and those of us who wanted the Church to 'grow' should ignore or outright oppose his teaching. Through grace, the Holy Spirit began inspiring within me a great love for, and obedience to, the Holy Father. I needed to ask forgiveness for my gullibility and grant forgiveness for the betrayal I had received at the hands of these Church leaders and educators.

The end of each video session featured the writings of Catherine Doherty, the foundress of Madonna House, whose writings I had read in my youth, but had forgotten over the years. Moved by her words, I decided to do more spiritual reading, and armed with many new books, including papal writings, I began to read voraciously. By this time, little Celeste had arrived, and our long, frequent nursing sessions afforded me many opportunities to read. My education took the first real strides it had had in years, without me leaving my doorstep, or children, to gain it.

As I read one book after another, I was astonished at how everything in my life appeared to come together. I seemed to be emerging from a thick, stale fog to discover the fresh air of truth and freedom. Despite the excitement of this new knowledge, something essential still lacked: my own faith in God. I knew I needed to pray, but in my newfound zeal I often, erroneously, succumbed to the temptation to postpone prayer and spend all my time reading, like a parched man too busy studying about water to get a drink.

Catherine Doherty led me to the Water: her love of God and the Church, her wisdom, faith and plain common sense spoke powerfully to me. Her 'Little Mandate', the humble, hidden way, beckoned: perhaps I could find fulfilment down this unassuming road. But at what cost? Only my pride, my selfishness and my irrational fears, which I'd clung to all these years. God's grace gave me the courage and the desire to put them aside and step into the unknown, into the arms of Christ.

Ralph Martin was the author who made me think. In *Hungry for God: Practical Help in Personal Prayer*, he spoke of spiritual reading as an 'aid, not a substitute', for prayer, and added that busyness or a perceived lack of time were poor excuses for avoiding prayer.

In the hectic weeks following Celeste's birth, I'd committed these errors, postponing my much-needed encounter with the living God. One passage in *Hungry for God* spoke of seeing the potential for prayer-time in all of our quiet everyday tasks, giving, as one example, the time spent rocking and nursing a baby. Engaged in that very activity as I read those words, I sheepishly put the book down and began to pray.

I wanted to know Christ intimately again and invited him back into my heart. I rededicated my life to him, and put my future into his hands – or at least acknowledged that it had been there all along. I placed my trust in him, giving him all my worries, fears, hopes and aspirations.

When you offer all you have to the Lord, he removes some things forever, gives others back a hundredfold and keeps yet others until the time is right. Somehow you don't miss what is gone, you find greater joy in what he gives back and as for those things still in his hands, you simply needn't spend time and energy fretting about them. This is the case in my life.

Embracing my vocation and striving to be obedient to God's will has made a tremendous difference to me and my family. The consuming desire to return to school, my feelings of dissatisfaction with life and resentment towards my family have disappeared. These have been replaced with peace, joy and the ability to do small, even distasteful, tasks well for love of God. I have begun to experience a deeper communion with the Lord and the thrill of answered prayers. I love my children even more now and appreciate them as a precious gift from God. My relationship with Dan has blossomed and borne more fruit in the delightful person of Geneva, who arrived twenty-one months after Celeste. Never before could I have admitted – especially in print – that I am proud to call myself a wife, mother and homemaker.

Christ has set me free: free from the expectation to succeed by the world's standards, free from the oppression of a self-centred life, free to enjoy all the gifts of godly womanhood that the world would have us deny. I am free to love, serve and obey Christ and his Church, by serving him every day, right where I am.

Lest this begin to sound idyllic, let me hasten to add that our family is not without its share of difficulties in general, and awful days in particular. Unfortunately, accepting my vocation did not automatically make me a patient mother or a good cook. Home-schooling presents a variety of challenges, Dan's job situation remains tenuous and I must daily combat my inclination towards laziness and disorganisation.

If I have learned anything in the last several years, it is that without God I can do nothing, and the life of faith is a life of total reliance upon his grace. I have also accepted that I do not need a printed 'MA' behind my name to feel important, for the Lord values me simply because I am his child. I praise him and thank him for his wisdom, love and generosity in having bestowed upon me that unseen degree, the 'double MA', which every mother, even the Queen of Heaven, is privileged to possess: MAMA to my children. His graces and gifts comprise the only 'Master's' degree that I will ever need. Thank you, Master.

Two

My Pink T-Shirt

by Catherine Fournier

Last night, while doing one final chore before turning in – putting away clean laundry piled on my bed – I came across a t-shirt. It's a pink t-shirt with a printed message, sent to me as a Christmas present by my friend Valerie. When I finally had the laundry put away, I climbed into bed, thinking about that t-shirt.

I met Valerie in my first year at university. She and I sat beside each other in maths class and played pranks on the professor. He was one of those earnest mid-thirty types who wanted to be our 'pal'. We drew cartoons on our assignments, sat quietly at the back of the class with pencils sticking out of our ears and tossed paper aeroplanes out of the windows. We didn't really disrupt the class, and since we were at the top of the class as far the work went, there was nothing poor Barry could do. He wanted us to call him Barry.

I had never had a friend like Valerie before, someone smart and serious about school work, but with a convoluted sense of humour like mine. High school can be a bleak time in the 'no man's land' between the scholastic always-serious nerds and the time-passing, never-serious clowns. We blossomed in each other's friendship, and have remained close friends ever since, despite our different paths in life. Valerie mastered the alchemy of chemistry and went on to pursue a degree in Bio-physical Chemistry. I realised at the end of first year that chemistry was a mysterious realm to which I had no intellectual passport, and transferred to Arts, intending to earn a degree in History.

By the time Valerie had her Honours degree and first job, I had two babies, a small house and a severe post-natal depression. By the time she had her first promotion and first apartment in a trendy part of town, I had three children and my husband finally had a regular job. By the time she moved to a senior position in a government agency, I had four children, a town house, my father was dying of cancer and since my mother and sisters were splitting at the seams, I was the stretched band-aid holding the extended family together.

Five years ago when Valerie moved across the country for a higher employment opportunity, I had five children, was home schooling and building a house in the country. All my time was spent working for or thinking about my husband and children. Valerie was involved in political parties, had a wide network of friends and a busy social life. Three years ago, when she came home for a visit, I had six children, a nearly finished house in the country and in my rare hours of free time, the beginnings of a career in freelance writing. In order to have an undisturbed conversation, Valerie and I went for a walk.

I had always secretly envied Valerie's life. Her apartment was neat, tidy and quiet. She had nice clothes and a leather armchair. She went out to dinner, planned surprise parties, knew how to deal with any social situation and her interesting job actually contributed to society. She was a woman with the kind of life that feminists said we all wanted and deserved. I compared myself to Valerie, always felt like a throwback and questioned the satisfaction I had found in my life. Was I fooling myself?

Mind you, Valerie didn't have a husband or any children. Engaged for many years, she eventually realised that while her intended enjoyed the convenience of a fiancée, he had no intention of taking on the responsibilities of a wife. I could understand that she was occasionally lonely and frustrated by her lack of family, but I still thought that perhaps she had chosen the more satisfying path.

'Oh, Cat', she wailed, trudging through the January snow. 'I look at you and your children and I realise – I've wasted my life! I might never have children; I've completely wasted my time. You were right!'

It is not often that one sees down 'the road not taken', but that is what I was given that cold winter afternoon: an opportunity to see what I might have become. In all my struggles, with my conversion, with prayer, with pride, with NFP, with surrendering myself to the duty of the moment, with trust in God, with family troubles, even with having 'so many kids', I have always *felt* I was on the right path, but I've never *known*. I couldn't say anything to make Valerie feel better, I could only listen.

Last summer, my best friend Valerie married an absolute sweetheart of a man she met a year ago. Early last spring, I baked her wedding cake as I promised I would many years ago. She too now knows that she was on the right path, or she never would have met Don. At last report, they are looking for a house and talking about having children.

And this Christmas, she mailed me a t-shirt. It reads, 'If Mama ain't happy ain't nobody happy'.

Now, at first glance, the phrase sounds like a threat, 'I will be fulfilled, then I will take care of you guys'. And this may have been the sense that Valerie meant when she sent it to me. Her independent life has made it difficult for her to understand my entangled life, that it can be *okay* to put others' needs first. She worries about my health and she's always telling me to take care of myself, not to let my family take me for granted. Last year, she sent me a small box of gourmet chocolates with strict instructions that I was to eat them myself – don't tell Valerie, I shared them with Peter. I don't mind her prodding; I figure friends are supposed to look out for each other, and chocolates or a rarely worn pink t-shirt are fairly harmless.

'If Mama ain't happy ain't nobody happy' is a message I can interpret in a Catholic way. Most modern day propaganda *says* the right words but *means* the wrong things. Just think about it: does the National Action Committee on the Status of Women mean the same thing by the word 'freedom' as Mother Teresa? Does NATO mean the same thing by 'peace' that Christ did? How about 'equality', 'responsible', or 'life'? Even the word 'marriage' is misused.

So, let's think about the word 'mother', or 'mama', for a minute. Nowadays, we have biological mothers and surrogate mothers, birth mothers and adoptive mothers, working mothers, single mothers, foster mothers, honorary mothers, the Earth mother and on and on. Women are more, our modern rhetoric insists, more than breeding vessels for the next generation.

And modern rhetoric is right. Women are more than bodies in which to grow babies. Having this one idea right, predictably, off the rhetoricians run in all the wrong directions. 'Women need to find fulfilment beyond having children', they proclaim, 'they need opportunities outside the home!' If children could raise themselves, this proclamation would be a possibility.

How about the word 'happy'? We would all like to be happy, but what does 'happy' mean? Here again, modern thought is partially right; happiness is a personal responsibility, you have to be happy on your own, no one can make you happy.

Again, off go modern thinkers, leaping over hedges and ditches in the pursuit of happiness, crying, 'What ever makes you happy is right! Don't let anything or anyone stand in the way of your personal happiness!' And, if immortal souls weren't involved, their recommendations would probably work.

Happiness is not simply and solely a personal responsibility. It isn't found in the solitary pursuit of satisfaction or success, turning inward for strength and denying the moral consequences or repercussions of individual actions. We have immortal souls, an eternal relationship with God, and responsibilities and obligations as a result.

Beside my kitchen sink, stuck underneath the window casing, are two little cards. On one, a quote from Saint Augustine, 'Thou hast made us O Lord for thyself, and our heart shall find no rest until it rest in Thee'. And the second, a quote by Georges P Vanier,

19th Governor General of Canada, 'We all have to fall in love with someone – Why not God? And through Him with our neighbour'. This is happiness; knowing who we are, who we belong to, and what we have been given to do.

But what does this have to do with my t-shirt? What does happiness in service to my family have to do with it? How can I agree that 'If Mama ain't happy, ain't nobody happy'?

Are there some people who leap joyfully, wholeheartedly and completely into the role marriage made for them? Is it only me and my generation that has had to struggle with the conflicting messages between divine, moral and natural law, and modern secular society? Or does everyone to some extent have to struggle with the transition from childish *me* to adult *we*? While Valerie was studying, learning and working, I was working and learning too. It didn't come easily, but I eventually learned that the only way to place my family at the centre of my life was to place myself at the centre of my family.

A mother is at the heart, or the centre of a family, because while she is honoured by her family as the queen of her household, both the children and husband constantly turn to her for love, life, guidance, inspiration, prayers, advice, food, attention, in a word: *mothering*. We all know that if a heart, the centre of the body, beats weakly, or irregularly, and does not effectively and properly do the job it is made to do, the body becomes sick. We need to also recognise that if a mother does not mother effectively, placing herself at the centre of her family and doing what she is made to do, the family will become unhealthy.

Since she is at the centre, the health, atmosphere or personality of the family is determined by and radiates from, the mother. What she is, the rest of the family is. And since happiness is not separate from our role and relationship to others, but is found in those roles and relationships, it is a condition, not a prerequisite of motherhood. What she feels, the rest of the family feels. Mama doesn't have to be happy first, Mama has to be happy being Mama. Then everybody else will be happy.

Three

Miracles Along the Way

by Dianne Fuller

The social worker was pleased to tell me that she had a baby for us. We had asked for a Native Canadian baby when we heard that there was a shortage of adoptive homes for them.

'But there's a problem', she said. 'He may not be adoptable because his shoulder blades touch in the back'.

A few days later, the social worker phoned again to say that for some inexplicable reason, the baby's shoulder blades no longer touched. We made arrangements to bring Paul home on the eve of the Feast of Saints Peter and Paul. We chose the name when we applied to adopt a baby boy six months earlier in 1967, in honour of our devotion to Saint Paul.

Paul wasn't our first baby. When we brought him home to our hobby farm, he met his two older brothers, David, two and a half years old, and Robbie, a year and a half old. Since we had always hoped to adopt at least one child, we decided this was an opportune time.

As a registered nurse, I puzzled over the 'touching and un-touching' of Paul's shoulder blades. There was no medical explanation for it. I concluded that it must be Saint Paul working miracles for us, and thanked him for his intercession.

Over the next ten years, our family expanded to include Marie and Tom. Our family needed another girl, as males significantly outnumbered the females. Since I was having difficulty carrying pregnancies to term, we attempted to adopt another child. The social worker responded, 'Definitely not'. We already had five children and there was a waiting list.

In 1976, after losing another baby, we applied again. At that time, more Catholic babies were available due to a lower abortion rate among Catholic women. On our application questionnaire, we indicated openness to accept a 'hard to place' child with almost any handicap, deafness excepted. My husband, Roy, felt very strongly that we shouldn't take a deaf baby. Our farm would be too dangerous for a child who couldn't hear.

Several months later the social worker called. 'We have an eleven month old baby we would like to tell you about. Come and look at the pictures of her and see what you think. We aren't sure if she is adoptable. She is deaf'.

Due to nerve damage, Teresa had a profound hearing loss and would never hear sounds softer than loud drum beats. In spite of our reservations, we could not refuse this child. And so Teresa became our sixth.

Shortly before accepting Teresa, I had endeavoured to address an allergy to cow's milk in our family. We acquired several milk goats, and I began to serve the children goat's milk. After Teresa had been with us for about a week, she showed indications of hearing. I phoned the social worker and asked, 'If I tell you she's not deaf will you tell me you are going to take her back?'

Of course he wouldn't.

Teresa's hearing tests were normal. Her deafness was caused by an allergy to cow's milk and since she had been with us, she'd had only goat's milk. Another miracle! Unfortunately, because Teresa was unable to hear for her first year of life, her language and listening skills lagged far behind that of her peers. As she grew older it became apparent that she had severe learning disabilities. She couldn't seem to understand things very easily, and yet she had a great sense of humour.

In 1982, when Teresa was six years old, she became obsessed with the idea of having a baby sister. At forty years old, I bemusedly consoled her, 'I don't need another baby, Teresa. You are my baby'. After several months of this exchange, I started to waver, thinking that maybe we should have another baby. Even though I would probably have to spend the first few months in bed, I could supervise the children from the couch. Our oldest was eighteen years old, and the children were all well able to cook and clean. Even so, under the circumstances, another baby was probably not very wise.

One Friday evening in January 1982, we were surprised by a phone call from a social worker. Unsure of how to broach the subject, she apologised, but assured me that she had permission from the Minister of Human Resources to contact us. She continued, 'The mother of your adopted daughter has just had a baby. Since we like to keep siblings together, we were wondering if you would be willing to adopt the baby. Could we please let her know by Monday?' The idea of adoption hadn't crossed our minds; we were past the age of being considered and had six children.

After the initial shock, my husband Roy agreed that by Sunday night we would have to come to a decision. Over the years, Roy and I have developed a method of discernment. We discuss the situation thoroughly, being very honest about what we see as the consequences of possible decisions: 'We were about to be able to have more time without the children and do more with each other. Now we'll be starting over again. Do you realise that I could be collecting the family allowance and old age pension at the same time? What would it mean to Teresa to have her sister with her?'

After discussion, we pray that God's will be done. In our family prayers after supper, we include these problems and questions. Sometimes we say the rosary alone or together for a special intention. But most of the praying is just a constant plea while we are going about our usual activities. Whenever we think of the unresolved situation, we ask God to help us know his will. Often, I know what I would like, but Roy has not come to the same conclusion. When that happens, I tell him to decide after I am satisfied that he understands what I think. While he is deciding I pray for God's will.

By Sunday night, we had come to the conclusion that seven children would be a good family size for us.

We arrived at the hospital to collect Catherine when she was ten days old. As soon as I saw her, I was sure she was a Down Syndrome baby. I reached for her tiny hand and saw the tell-tale transverse crease on her palm. I immediately thought of Paul and Teresa. Paul's shoulder blades touched in the back, and then they didn't. Teresa was deaf, and then she wasn't. Who was I to argue whether this baby was or was not a Down Syndrome baby? I didn't mention my suspicion to anyone, and after a few weeks, didn't even think of it.

When we brought Catherine home, I couldn't help thinking how God spoils me. He gives me whatever I want. I don't even have to ask him. As I marvelled about God's great goodness to me, I slowly realised my thinking was a bit backwards. God set me up; it was his idea first and somehow he instilled the desire in me. Teresa had certainly been persistent in the campaign for a baby sister. God knew her little sister needed a home. As a result, I again experienced the joy of being the mother of a new baby.

A year later, two people independently told me that they had been very upset at their first sight of Catherine. They believed at the time that she had Down Syndrome, and I didn't seem to be aware of it. Now, they confessed their mistake; she didn't look like a Down Syndrome child. As Catherine grew older, I could no longer find the transverse crease. Since Down Syndrome is a chromosomal anomaly, the crease shouldn't have disappeared. Maybe I was wrong.

Although Catherine does not have Down Syndrome, she does have severe behaviour problems and learning disabilities. She is very probably a victim of foetal alcohol exposure. Catherine arrived with a tragic inheritance, and in her brokenness, I see the suffering of Christ. This innocent child, through no fault of her own, bears the burden of her ancestors, of our humanity. She is subjected to the ridicule, scorn and rejection of the ones in society who, through no merit of their own, are 'normal'. Her wild behaviour resulting from the inability to control herself has caused enormous distress to herself, to our family, and her social contacts.

Yet, the miracles continue. Foetal alcohol syndrome is said to be incurable, but Catherine has improved beyond our wildest hopes. The C.A.L.L., Centre for the Advancement of Listening and Language, in Regina, Saskatchewan, has helped both Catherine and Teresa. Over a two year period, from 1990 to 1992, we have made the 3000 kilometre trip to Regina ten times. It has been well worth the effort.

At the C.A.L.L. Centre, the Tomatis Method is used to enhance listening. High frequency sounds, similar to those heard by the unborn child in the womb, enable the muscles in the inner ear to redevelop, causing many positive changes in the child. When the sounds the child hears change from the prenatal sounds through liquid amniotic fluid to the sounds the child hears after birth through the medium of the air, the 'sonic birth' occurs. Because the sounds used during the programme are the recorded sounds of the mother reading a story to the child, a new closeness and bonding between the mother and child occurs after the sonic birth. This is especially important for adopted children.

Teresa had always been a happy child, not overly concerned about her adoption. As soon as she underwent the sonic birth, she began to ask questions about her birth parents. On our way home from Regina after the sonic birth, and after talking about the learning disabilities her birth mother experienced, she announced 'When I grow up, I'm going to find my birth mother and take her to Regina so they can help her too!'

Teresa was in grade 8, reading at a grade 2 level, when she began the Tomatis program. By grade 10, her reading level improved by five grades to a grade 7 level and she continues to improve. She has happily remarked, 'Before, in grade 8, I could only read Dr Seuss books. Now I can read novels!'

The C.A.L.L. programme has also made a tremendous difference in Catherine. She is much calmer and better able to control her behaviour. As a result, our family life has returned almost to normal, after nine years of agony and frustration.

A friend of our family who is a priest, understanding the suffering that Catherine brought with her, asked me, 'Would you have adopted her if you had known what you would have to go through?' And before I could answer he implored, 'Oh, Diane, say that you would!'

I have often pondered that question. Many people have told me how 'lucky' Catherine is that we adopted her. A Catholic sister once said to me, 'You've rescued her from the garbage dump!' When I think of Catherine, I realise that it could have just as easily been me with all the problems and Catherine in the position to adopt. What would I have done if she hadn't adopted me? If we are unwilling to suffer for each other, how seriously are we really taking our commitment to Christ?

The answer to Father's question was, 'Yes, I would take her again because I love her'.

I have learned many important lessons because of our adopted children. One of the most important is of God's great love for these children. They, in their innocence, bear the cost of the inhumanity that humanity has inflicted. We must trust that God in his compassion will lead us to the solutions we need. And we need not be surprised at a few miracles along the way.

Four

At a Disadvantage

by Geraldine Hertz

The low point of my life was the morning I trudged down the stairs to find my four preschoolers chirping like young robins, totally unaware of the bedlam surrounding them. I poured myself a cup of coffee from the urn I'd prepared the night before, obligingly plugged in by my thirteen year old before she left for school.

I took a long, steady swallow of the bitter brew and looked around me, not wanting to believe what I saw. I was appalled at the mess. They'd made cocoa and waffles. Someone spilled his glass of cocoa and another had walked through it, and then rushed for the school bus, leaving a clearly definable, sticky trail across the kitchen I'd mopped and waxed the night before. Someone spilled the waffle batter and a child had walked though that!

I set my coffee cup down and cried. As I wept, all the sad events of the past months swept over me in a depressing cloud of misery. My father lay dying in the hospital several hundred miles away. I'd just come home, exhausted, from the ordeal of staying with my mother during his brain surgery for cancer. As I thought of him, my heart tightened with pain, and I sobbed in agony.

The doorbell rang. Glancing at my face in a nearby mirror, I hurried to the door. But that one quick glance at my red nose and puffy eyes shrivelled my dignity. My fair and freckled face had turned red from crying, and I was a mess. Still, what did I care? How could I care, with my father dying?

I opened the door to see the man who held the mortgage on

our home. He checked with us once a year to see what we'd been doing with the building. I put one nervous hand to my uncombed hair and tried to imagine what he would think of the mess, but the thought stifled me. As I opened my mouth to apologise, I recalled a quotation from Hamlet, 'The lady doth protest too much, methinks'.

Frankly, nine in the morning was no time for Shakespeare. I resented him and this man who stood before me staring around in disbelief. When I'd asked him for money to build the house several months before, he asked how many children we had.

'Twelve', I answered.

'I have only two', he answered coolly. 'I want mine to have every advantage'.

I rose to his bait. 'That depends on what you mean by advantages', I answered. 'I want mine to have a warm home, and lots of love'.

He had wisely changed the subject, but now here he was. I looked at him and was stricken dumb by my own state of affairs, and for a moment I'd gladly have crawled under the bed to hide. This man, whom I'd thought so cold, looked at me with sympathy that I could hardly believe.

'What's wrong?' he asked. 'Did I come at a bad time?'

Sobbing, I waved him inside and sat down. He handed me a generous tissue from his pocket and waited for me to speak.

'It's – it's my dad. He's got cancer, and he's dying', I sobbed. 'I just can't get things done when I think of him'.

'I should think not', he answered, and began to chat about trivial matters until I lost my feeling of mortal shame and the tears dried on my cheeks. I remembered my manners long enough to pour him a cup of coffee, and I had another myself.

By the time he left, I had begun to believe, if not in myself, at least in the kindness he'd extended to me. I had not exactly shown him the advantages of having a large family, but he'd forgiven my mess, at least.

It's a good thing babies can laugh and coo because nothing else would have cured me that day. After the baby had his morning bath, and I'd fed and burped him, I could tell myself that it didn't really matter about the world out there. I'd built my own world within these walls, and that was all that counted.

Besides, rushing about trying to please the neighbours was a much more sterile way to go. At least with my children, I could face God and know that the heritage of faith was extended to them. Not even their busy father could give them the time and the attention that was mine to give. I alone saw the children blossom with the love of God and knew that I'd been showing them the way to him.

Other advantages are there in abundance too.

College? They can have it if they work for it. Mine did.

Money? It can be earned.

New clothes? So sew a little.

Rich food? Who needs it? The feminine figure is trim today.

Fast car? We want our kids in heaven, but later!

Nowhere are the advantages good enough to trade for a single child's soul. God is good to mothers. They don't have to be super-intelligent. They don't have to be eager-beavers for work. The work will sit there and wait, I'm here to tell you! They don't have to be anything but themselves, loving their babies and teaching them their prayers.

I'm sure that our Lord's mother went ahead with her work even when at a disadvantage, without seeking acclaim from the world. As mothers, and as her followers, our job is to love enough, that the tender encircling of our care round our little ones is an invisible shield against the rebuffs of a cold world. Our confidence and warmth give them a living image of the strength and wisdom of God. By our love we teach our children that without love there is nothing; if we have God, nothing else matters.

Five

My Child is Handicapped

by Debbie Park

I'm feeling pain tonight – crawled out of bed to write. All week, a heaviness and unhappiness has been weighing in my heart. I found myself angry at those around me, my helpers, my son's helpers, my husband, children, mother, friends and God. I didn't know there was pain inside.

I should recognise the symptoms by now. It's not the first time this cycle has occurred where somehow I suppress little pains here and there. I don't bring them to Jesus. I forget them and they become stuffed inside and one builds on top of another. Outwardly I am not aware of an inner pain, but I am aware of anger. I am aware that I feel deadened inside and lack joy. I am aware of a darkness and heaviness in my soul. It builds until finally the frustration in me seeks relief. I see now in the last weeks I tried to give myself comfort in food, in people, in shopping, in nostalgic thoughts, but nothing made the tension ease.

Finally, tonight, I give Jesus permission to bring out whatever he wanted. I began to be aware of pain, accumulated little pains. I feel the need to cry and be comforted. I suddenly desire to open my heart full of pains to Jesus and let him comfort me. I slip into bed beside my sleeping husband and I let my heart and mind picture Jesus. I begin talking to him in silent conversation. My heart talks to his heart.

'Jesus, again this pain has come up over Ben's handicaps. At times he seems so handicapped and at other times he looks so normal. But tonight, Jesus, I see his handicaps. They're painful to see, Jesus.'

I feel Christ's comforting embrace as my heart opens up to him. I try to listen, to hear his responses. Tears, waves of pain and images wash over me. I feel a relief of tension as the anger oozes out. I picture my head on Jesus' chest and feel his arms holding me. Images flash before me and I give them to him. Images of cross country skiing and wondering how we can do it now with Ben. Images of his long body growing longer, heavier, of carrying him from the chair to the car or to the rug and wondering if he will ever sit on his own. Images of looking at him in the bathtub – he's lying on his back, unable to sit, twenty months old, and I'm leaning over to lift him out and feeling the heaviness twisting my back. But I love him so.

Oh God. Right now I am in so much pain. My nose is running, my chest is heaving, tears stream down my face. I love him so. He is so beautiful. Is love ever without pain? With love, it hurts, yet it's always worth loving.

Oh, Ben, am I crying over my losses or yours? The Lord gave us emotions and wants us to be intimate with him, to bring to him all that is within us, to empty ourselves into him, so as not to carry heavy burdens. I truly have been unburdened tonight as I released my pains to Jesus and allowed myself to see him comfort and accept me. Even this is an act of will, to choose to let God comfort us.

So often I hear Jesus say, 'Open your heart to me. Let me comfort you'. The words are strange to me. I honestly don't know how to open my heart to the Lord. Gradually he is teaching me: bring me your sufferings, pains, joys, excitements, everything. Tell me about them. Share them with me that I may be part of your life. Let me heal where healing is needed. Let me listen to you.

Now that the pain is released, I feel lightness and a return of joy. Thank you, Jesus. I know tomorrow will look brighter and I'll be able to enjoy my children and family and feel at peace with God.

The mystery of Jesus has touched me again. I can't see him, can't physically touch him, can't outwardly hear him. I have to choose to believe that he's here. When I do, and let myself be held by him, I'm refreshed and given new life. Sometimes, because of the physical handicap of not seeing Jesus, I can allow myself to doubt his existence. But when I choose to believe, I'm moved.

I want to share the beauty of Ben. This child, to whom God has granted life in the face of death, affects our family and hearts over and over. So often in my busy days, when my mind has been full of duties, I pick him up, and he smiles this big, radiant smile that stretches across his face and into his eyes. Suddenly in my busyness I too am laughing and smiling, and I become aware of God.

Ben, this handicapped child, whose condition makes so many demands on me, comforts and blesses me with his spirit and heart. His gentleness, his acceptance of all he undergoes, his continual cheerfulness speak to me of love, of God.

'God, give me a grateful heart', I once prayed earnestly.

Ben has taught me gratitude. I grow thankful for little improvements. I'm learning patience. I'm grateful for things I took for granted, such as eating food with one's mouth. I never thought crawling or sitting were gifts before they were absent in Ben. Sight. I always had good sight and assumed my children would too. Ben wears glasses. Even breathing is a gift. Ben struggled for breath in his first year of life. He teaches me perseverance. He never gives up. He keeps going and trying.

Something different is growing in my heart. Trust. I've had a lot of difficulty with trust. I've prayed endlessly for Ben's healing. I always wanted it to be quick but God is showing me how to quietly trust in him. To wait and believe, to not give up and yet to be content with the present without knowing God's full intent. I find a peace pervading my desire for Ben's healing, a joy and love for the way he is, and yet faith that God is healing him in his way and in his time.

Yes, Ben is handicapped. He is handicapped in outward ways, but don't we all possess some advantage when we compare ourselves to others? Our handicaps are just less visible. Ben has taught me to look deeper at life and to see the heart and soul first. May God be praised for his great gift to us through Benjamin.

Six

I am Third

by Catherine Fournier

Every morning I wade into my little boys' room to make their beds and tidy away the tangle of pyjamas, toys and rolled-up-wads that barely resemble socks. Buried in this stirred together mess, I find a small black and white stuffed cow. An insignificant object with a significant history.

My husband is a very romantic man. He may not appear so to the casual observer. For one thing, he's tall and he gangles. In blue jeans, he looks like a logger; in a shirt and tie he looks stern and imposing, a minion of bureaucracy. For another, he doesn't express his romanticism in ways that anyone reared on conventional notions of romance would recognise. He's never read a Harlequin Romance, or watched a soap opera. He thinks Valentine's Day is stupid, has a hard time understanding birthday gifts. When we were courting, he preferred a ten mile walk to a movie or dinner. Every time.

When I hinted that a gift of fruit or flowers would be appropriate after the birth of our first child, he returned two hours later with a brown paper grocery bag. In the bag was a bunch of daffodils from our own garden wrapped in damp paper towels and a bowl of washed and cut strawberries, nested in another bowl of crushed ice. Not exactly what I had in mind, but you must agree there was more effort and thought in his offering.

So, on the crisp autumn afternoon three years ago at the county fair when he lined up his quarters and announced he was going to win me a prize, I could hardly breathe for shock. A conventional romantic gesture!

We visit Madonna House, the community and retreat centre, in Combermere often. We have good friends there, it's a pleasant visit and a valuable lesson, a glimpse into another life, one more focused and directed than ours, distracted and tugged as we are by school, work and the duty of the moment.

There, every door has a hand printed sign above it. In simple calligraphy, the signs announce, 'I am Third'. An entire philosophy is summed up in those three words: God first, my neighbour second and finally myself. Love, service, knowledge – I am Third. An easy message to understand intellectually. One we are all called to grasp with the whole of our lives. This is not as easy.

The midway game at the fair involved rolling a large metal ball along a track, hard enough that it would go over one hump but gently enough that it would come to rest at the top of the next hump and not come rolling down again. It required a careful gauging of weight, momentum and your own strength. Each turn cost a quarter.

After three dollars, Peter succeeded. The ball stayed at the top of the hump, and a light went on. He needed five lights to get the prize. He kept rolling. Two more dollars and another light came on. I had been standing a little distance away, to give him more room to move, to intercept the children who might distract him. But now, I stepped closer.

'Pete, you don't have to do this; spend the money on something else'.

'I said, I'm going to win you a prize', he replied, his eyes on the ball, 'and I'm going to. Now be quiet'.

After that, he won twice in a row. He had four lights on, and about twelve quarters left. The children, bored, wandered away to the next booth, where a young man showed them how to throw bean bags at a wall of trap doors. Two went over to the booth across the aisle, sniffing deeply at the scent of fresh hotdogs. Peter continued to heft the heavy metal balls and roll them up the ramp.

One, two . . . five, six . . . nine, ten.

On his last quarter, the ball stayed at the top. The last light came on, all the lights flashed and bells rang. The din was hardly noticeable against the background noise of the midway, but it seemed like fireworks and a brass band to me. My husband, my hero, my knight, had won me a prize! I stood grinning as the barker, fat and loud in a striped shirt and pork pie hat, came over to Peter.

My husband and our oldest daughter, Tina, have a very special friendship. He is always a firm and guiding father, but at this same time, she has a permanent kink in her little finger from wrapping her daddy around it. Peter left for a summer's work when Tina was barely three weeks old. The evening he came home, after hugging me, he asked to see the baby. With the experience of four months, I lifted her sleeping from the crib and handed her to Peter sitting cross-legged in the centre of our bed. He gazed intently at the little bundle, breathed 'ohhh' softly, and dropped her.

It was another four months before baby Tina would permit him to hold her again, a punishment he felt richly deserved. We still tease him about this. Tina has made a game of lifting her eyebrows and purring 'Daaaddy?' Peter laughs helplessly and takes out his wallet or the car keys. 'I know I can get him to do anything I want', she says, 'and I'm careful never to take advantage of it'.

All of Peter's children are dear to him in a way that can't be expressed in words, only in the way he lives his life, makes them the reason for every action. This surely is the mark of a truly romantic man, he loves his children as he loves their mother, with every thought and deed.

The barker handed over his microphone at the same time, 'We have a winner here, a winner, a winner! See how easy it is to win a prize, right this way, win a prize!'

As Peter took the toy and turned away from the counter, Tina – tall, smiling, little finger ready – materialised at his elbow.

'You won a cow!' she exclaimed. 'I've always wanted one of those. Thank you, Dad!' And she kissed him on the cheek. Peter looked briefly bewildered, then smiled. 'You're welcome, Tina,' he said, looking over her shoulder at me, barely two feet away.

I had only a moment to be confused and indignant, *Hey! Wait a minute! That was mine!* to realise, *oh, I can't destroy this*, and then very amused, *well, talk about I am Third!* before Tina noticed me standing behind her.

'Congratulations Peter!' I kissed him on the cheek too. 'That's a cute cow, Tina.'

When my children were infants, it was very easy to put my needs and desires aside. They were so tiny, and so helpless, how could I deny them? Besides, their cry is designed by our wise and loving Heavenly Father to be the most distressing and un-ignorable thing in the world. They slept and ate, messed their diapers and finally smiled at all my silly faces. I told myself, 'So you haven't had a decent sleep in months; it's not like they do it on purpose'.

As they grew, putting my needs aside grew a little harder. The children were so insistent and demanding. Couldn't they wait just a minute? I knew very well that they could dress themselves and that they understood what *no* meant. Did I have to say it again! Balancing the duties of husband, house and children could all get to be a bit much.

'Still, they are just kids. If they trample all over my pride and patience, drown out my thoughts with theirs, interrupt every blessed thing I start, they honestly don't know they're doing it'. The main joy of childhood is the self-absorbed confidence that, yes indeed, they are the centre of the universe. And who are we to tell them differently? 'Besides', I would remind myself, 'it isn't going to last forever. Soon they'll be taking care of themselves, then I can call myself my own again.' In the meantime, I enjoyed watching them play. Teaching and training them was a constant challenge, a hug here and an admonition there, the tools of my trade of motherhood.

Eventually, they grew to the teen years. They looked like adults, they sounded like adults, sometimes they even thought like adults. They didn't cry when they were hungry – they just invaded my fridge and helped themselves – and they certainly didn't need my help with zippers anymore. I found myself growing impatient as they needed less and less physical attention and more and more mental attention. I struggled with the realisation that service to my children was becoming much harder, that it required more conscious thought, more thinking time, more love, not less as I had anticipated. The moment at the county fair, watching as, almost in slow motion, my daughter took the prize won for me, revealed both the problem and its solution.

The first problem was it wasn't just a cow I was losing. The cow represented my loss of Peter's personal attention. It wasn't the first time either. When the kids were young, evenings were our time, our private time together for talking and joking, for the sharing of the ideas and ideals that made our marriage. But now that they were older they could stay up with Peter long after I, tired, went to bed. In little ways, we didn't have much left for 'just us'. Peter and the children watched movies together that I didn't like. They had private jokes. They ate snacks that I had put aside for Peter and me. Jealously, selfishly, I didn't like it. I didn't want to share. Even with my children.

The second problem was that as Peter's wife and Tina's mother, I was losing myself too. Peter could not shatter his daughter's confidence that she was the centre of his universe and that, of course, he had won the prize for her. And neither could I. I had to set myself aside, and think about what she needed.

The solution wasn't easy. Getting up in the middle of the night, letting children climb all over me and step on my feet, reading *Tootle The Little Train* a hundred times, all the things I gave to my family that demanded my physical energy, was easy compared to putting my intangible self, my mind, wishes and personality aside. It was easy to know the right thing to do for my child because I loved and knew her. As her mother, it was easy to see what she needed at that moment. I know precisely her strengths and weaknesses. I know how she is growing, what she could be, what lessons and nurturing she still needs. What I had seen as a nice sentiment, an abstract statement, 'I am Third', suddenly came to life and bit me on the nose. Tina, Peter and then me. I really was Third.

Of course, realising that you are selfish and jealous – especially of your own children – and mentally lazy are not very comfortable revelations. I mentally filed the incident as an amusing story, and promptly forgot all about its larger implications. Except . . . have you ever noticed how some things just won't stay forgotten, and some lessons repeat themselves until you finally learn them?

I kept finding that cow around the house. I would find it lying tangled in dirty clothes and bed sheets in the boys' room, or underneath the living room couch, or in some corner of the back yard. In the midst of my frustration with perpetual household disorder, I kept recalling, I am Third. First God, then my family and then myself. They, Peter, Tina, Andrew, Sarah, Matthew, Jonathon and Robert, are my family, my vocation, my way to serve God. They have been entrusted to me and I love taking care of them. I am the only person who loves them and knows them this well, who can step aside for them and see what they need at this moment. The kind of service changes, but the nature of it never does and never will. It is always lovingly being Third. I learned that from a little black and white stuffed cow.

'I am Third' isn't an abstract notion, a bit of decoration over a doorway. Every 'neighbour' is my child, Mary's child and God's child. Of course, I *am* Third.

Seven

The Pilgrimage

by James G. Anderson

On the evening of 27 January, during a snow squall and a rather severe cold snap, the congregation of our domestic church was increased by one member, Malcolm, our second child. Stephen, our firstborn, was not yet two years old, and with his mother's arms occupied by 'another man', he had to rely more heavily upon his father for care and general entertainment.

Stephen and I began to take daily – or at least as the weather permitted, daily – walks to Saint Anne's, our local parish church, the steeple of which breaks over the knoll near our house. Our pilgrimage is not long. The walk takes less than ten minutes over the fields, but is lengthened when one is waylaid to inspect curious grasses and weeds, to swat at low-lying branches, imitate the crows' caws, and stare, wide-eyed, at the trucks that trundle around the bend and up the long hill on the road skirting the field we cross. Short legs make for a longer walk still, and while Stephen does nobly for being less than three feet tall, more often than not he would prefer the bird's eye view perched atop my shoulders. What an image we must strike, I often think – the Infant and Saint Christopher – as I wade from fence to fence.

Across the road, we pass through the tiny hamlet of Cormac, not more than a crossroad with Kitt's, its general store that serves also as post office and gas station, Saint Anne's and the rectory, a shrine to the grandmaternal saint that is the site of an annual pilgrimage, a half-dozen or so houses of varied vintage and size, a disused baseball diamond, the fading scoreboard which identifies it as having been once home to the Cormac Cardinals and a hockey rink. We cut the corner from the intersection through the churchyard and past a set of outdoor Stations of the Cross and an almost life-sized crucifix whose white-painted metal corpus bleeds rust from cracks in the knees and shins.

Entering the church, we remove our hats, mitts, backpack, and pause for a moment to catch our breath and absorb the solemnity and serenity of the Divine Presence that dwells beneath the red sanctuary lamp. Stephen enjoys the ritual of our visits to the Blessed Sacrament. He has learned the routine in general, our trip counter-clockwise around the inside of the church, and each visit I see that he acquires more of the specifics of devotion as we pause at each of our stations of adoration, veneration and education.

We make efforts to bless ourselves, liberally, at the holy water font upon entering. We venerate the relic of the parish's patroness, embedded in a priedieu before a statue of Our Lady of Fatima, with a kiss, which Stephen does by bowing to touch his nose to it with a click of his tongue. After a Hail Mary is prayed and a 'Good Saint Anne, pray for us!' uttered, we continue up the left side of the church to the tabernacle. Before his Majesty I kneel, my arms around my son who stands on the step in front of me, facing the Blessed Sacrament. Silently I hold up my family to Christ, and allow my son to bask in the rays of grace flowing from the Divine Mystery.

I have discovered that a gentle sway can extend our time of silent adoration to almost a full minute before Stephen starts to squirm and attempt to escape. Then it is to the statues and paintings that adorn the sanctuary and side altars: the Last Supper in relief on the altar, Jesus on the Cross, Saint Anne, Mary, Saint Joseph with the 'baby', Mary again, and finally, going up the right side to the back, the *Pietà*. Captivated by the glass eyes and the fact that the statue is within his reach, Stephen recites his litany of acquired anatomy – nose, eye, toe – as he points and pokes at the figures.

Beside the *Pietà* is a wrought iron rack of seven-day vigil candles. Once a week, Stephen takes coins from my hand and drops them carefully, one by one, into the metal offering box. We light a candle for the family, with a prayer, and with each visit through the week return to check its progress. If our visit is on a Friday, we make an abbreviated Stations of the Cross which are a little more than a Hail Mary and a pious thought before each image of the *Via*. This leads us back to the tabernacle.

The short pews along the side of the church in front of the tabernacle have only one end open, the other rests against the wall. One of these pews and a hymnal or two, affords Stephen a few minutes of contained amusement and myself a moment for prayer and reflection. I find myself wondering if these pilgrimages are entirely for Stephen's benefit after all. Perhaps they are more for my own? Certainly each visit is an opportunity to instruct my son in the Faith, young though he be, and to bring him to the Divine Presence. Yet am I not edified by the witness of my toddler son?

Indeed I am, strange as it may seem! I realise that the key aspects and elements of my faith are all mystery, and that faith is just that, believing in and responding to that which I cannot understand. And here you are, Stephen, my son, in your innocence and ignorance! Everything is mystery to you! You venerate the cross and relic of Saint Anne with your tongue-click kiss, you say 'Amen' to the prayers I pray, you stand still as long as you can in front of the tabernacle, and you have no understanding of why you do these things, except that it brings your father pleasure. You know only that you make me smile!

Undeniably, you bring both your father and your Father pleasure. Without any clue as to what you are doing, you bring down grace upon your family. Truly the child is the priest of the family, as a wise priest once told me. In your innocence you grant me a glimpse of the Father's love for me and his pleasure when I, faced by mystery, respond in faith. I recall the words of Catherine Doherty, 'Lord, grant me the heart of a child, and the awesome courage to live it out!'

I restore the hymnals to their right place, gather up Stephen with a kiss, and genuflect upon leaving the pew. As we make our way to the back of the church, if it is a sunny day, we may try to pick up the puddles and pools of stained light that lie on the carpet. After a final stop at the holy water and another wet semblance of the Sign of the Cross, Stephen and I don our outer clothes and I my back-pack.

We leave the church to retrace our steps through the church yard to Kitt's to pick up the mail and then across the road and fields for home, Stephen again settled on his perch. He makes encouraging noises and attempts forming words as we discuss the flora and fauna we pass, see and hear, what might be for lunch, and what Mommy and Malcolm are doing. And I think of Malcolm, of the day that he will join his father and elder brother on this pilgrimage and of what he will have to teach me.

Eight

Brent

by Richard Nibogie

Do not fear; only believe, and she shall be well. Luke 8:41-56.

My son Brent was twenty-five years old, tall, dark, and handsome. After a miscarriage of their first child, his twenty year old wife, Dawn, was now eight months pregnant.

Brent had been very healthy all his life. He managed to survive under the collapse of a brick wall at age seven, and overcame all the usual childhood diseases, bumps and scrapes. All of a sudden, however, his complexion turned grey. He endured chronic fatigue, night sweats and dramatic weight loss.

Brent consulted his doctor, who, after an examination and a few tests, diagnosed and treated him for low iron. After a month, Brent's health showed no signs of improvement. A month went by and his health did not improve; a tender lump had developed on his lower abdomen.

Concerned, the doctor examined Brent thoroughly and sent him to a cancer clinic for further tests. The test results verified that Brent had untreatable cancer of the liver. The doctors gave him one month to live. He and his wife, their parents, families and friends, were devastated.

The head surgeon of the cancer clinic promised to investigate the possibility of operating, but offered little hope for Brent's prognosis. His low blood level contributed to the twenty percent risk of bleeding to death on the operating table. His now swollen lymph nodes indicated that the cancer had progressed.

Therefore I tell you, whatever you ask in prayer, believe that you receive it, and you will. Mark 12:24.

My wife and I believed in prayer, and we had seen the power of prayer. Jesus performed miracles when he was on earth; he could perform one in our son's life. We would not accept defeat. We asked everyone we knew to pray for Brent's healing.

The Sunday before his operation, Brent stood before his church congregation to share this testimony: 'I've had a wonderful life and if God is calling me home, I'm ready to go'. He continued, 'I don't believe he's calling me home. Why would he bring me this far and not let me see my child born and grow up?' Brent asked for the congregation's continued prayers that he might be healed.

Dawn, who knew nothing of God prior to their courtship, confessed that night, 'It's been a good life with him. I'm proud to be carrying his child, and if the Lord is calling him home, I'm ready to let him go.' Although someone had urged her to give up all this 'spiritual stuff' and 'get real', she knew her spirituality was her strength in all this.

Dawn had accepted God's will. I struggled. I had my doubts that God would heal my son. I begged, I pleaded, I bargained. In the midst of this, a priest friend of ours came over to comfort us. He read from Hebrews 10 and 11, the chapters on faith. After he had finished, an unexplainable peace came over me. I resolved that I would accept whatever God had planned. I also prayed the scripture rosary with my wife, Trudy, which also seemed to soothe the pain we were feeling.

I clung to Matthew 21:21-22: *And Jesus answered them, 'Truly I say to you, if you have faith, and do not doubt, you shall not only do what was done to the fig tree, but even if you say to this mountain, "Be taken up and cast into the sea," it shall happen. And all things you ask in prayer, you shall receive if you have faith'.*

Instead of mountain I substituted cancer and prayed, 'Believe me, if you trust and do not falter and say to this cancer be lifted up and thrown from this body, it shall happen. You will receive all you pray for, provided you have faith.'

Our family prepared for the twelve hour operation. The surgeon expected to confirm the results after four hours in the operating room. If the doctors could not remove the cancer, they would stitch Brent up and send him home.

The operation progressed far better than expected. The physicians found the cancer was encased in the liver; it had not spread. Brent required five litres, rather than the standard six, of blood plasma for the operation. He still had enough good liver to sustain removal of the cancer. The doctors predicted that he would be incoherent for two to three days after the operation; he conversed coherently immediately after the operation. The doctors recommended that Brent be in an oxygen tent for two to three days; he did not require an oxygen tent. The doctors warned us that he would be in intensive care for two to three days and in the hospital for two to three weeks; he was out of intensive care the next day, the day after the operation he ate solid foods and walked. Brent was out of hospital in twelve days. The Sunday after his discharge, he again stood in front of his church congregation, this time as an answer to their prayers.

Although I was grateful for his healing, I could not understand why God chose to heal Brent while other parents' children were not healed. I am no better than anyone else. I am a sinner needing God's grace.

What shall we say then? Is there injustice on God's part? By no means! For he says to Moses, 'I will have mercy on whom I have mercy, and I will have compassion on whom I have compassion.' So it depends not upon man's will or exertion, but upon God's mercy. Romans 9:14-17.

My heart is full of gratitude for God's astounding power to heal. I have seen the words of Scripture fulfilled, 'Do not fear; only believe, and she shall be well'. Little did I realise to what extent our faith in God would be tested and strengthened. I thank God for answering our prayer.

I am constantly reminded that God is almighty. He is in control no matter what the situation may be. The crucial question for me is whether I believe this or not. God is always faithful to his word. In the past I have been fearful and close to despair. I now experience peace and joy, knowing that God's hand is on our lives. I have confidence. I am secure in knowing God's love is for all who turn to him and pray. I can trust him to keep any situation from becoming unendurable, for he has promised this and he will do what he says, and he will show me how I can bear up patiently.

On the day of his operation, Brent, six feet four inches tall, weighed 139 pounds. Nearly two years on, he could maintain his weight at 190, enjoy his job as a big-rig trucker, his wife and two children, nineteen-month William and six-month-old Courtney. There is no recurrence of the cancer. Brent believes he was healed because God has more for him to do. He will be faithful to that.

Nine

Our Son's Brush With Death

by Don Ellis

On 8 July, 1996, the youngest of our six children, seven year old John, rode his bicycle down a hill into the path of a truck. In the hours that followed, we believe we witnessed the power of prayer and the mercy of God.

In February 1996, our family had moved from Fort Smith, a little town in the Northwest Territories, to Yellowknife, a beautiful little city bounded by a bay of Great Slave Lake on one side and endless bush on the others. We rented when we first arrived, but by July, we had found a house to purchase.

We were already fixing up the house when we signed the mortgage at 1:00 pm on 8 July. John and his ten year old brother Isaac went out to discover the neighbourhood on their bicycles. I had just returned to work when my fourteen year old daughter Mary called and left a message, 'John's been hit by a truck. Go straight to the hospital.'

I ran to grab a taxi. On the way to the hospital, I passed the scene of the accident. John's bicycle was crumpled up beside the road, the front tire blown right off the frame. A small crowd looked sombre. I expected the worst: to find my dead son at the hospital. Instead, I alighted from the taxi at the hospital entrance to hear his screaming.

The ambulance crew had transferred John to a body board with a neck brace to prevent movement. He had been knocked unconscious at impact and now awake, had no idea what was happening. He hurt, he had been disfigured, his movement was constricted and he was terrified. He was already barely recognisable; I looked but couldn't see any teeth. He screamed and grabbed at the bloody neck brace.

John is a reasonable boy. When he suffered accidents, you could talk him down. This was another story. I asked John to trust me; he said he couldn't. He thought they were trying to strangle him. But he was alive. And he could speak. Good start.

Providentially, my wife Susan had bought him a new bicycle helmet the day before the accident. Without it, he would have died instantly, but through God's protection, he survived the initial impact. We were later told that a slightly different angle of impact would have killed him, and a split second difference in the timing of his descent would have put him under the truck's wheels.

Still, we worried now about brain damage. Screaming was a bad sign. Susan arrived as emergency staff began to peel away his clothes to assess additional damage. She immediately decided her forte was praying, not staring at her mangled son.

In the four hours that followed, John had no anaesthetic and swung between states of agitation and weariness. Concerned about head injury, the hospital staff couldn't let him sleep. We kept John awake and tried to reassure him. After receiving a Tylenol suppository, he calmed down and grew accustomed to the forest of tubes surrounding him.

Behind the scenes, unknown to us, friends and family began to mobilise a prayer network spanning three countries. We discovered, as if we need further proof, the power of prayer and what wonderful friends we had. All kinds of people, friends and some we didn't even know, phoned the kids at home to offer rides, food, money, any emergency assistance. The whole experience reminded us in a tangible way that we were very much enfolded by a caring community, both locally and internationally. Humbling, gratifying; it is many things to have a severe accident happen to your family, but mostly it's amazing. God finds helpers, sometimes people you've discounted.

The doctors decided to evacuate John to Edmonton, calling in the University of Alberta Paediatric Intensive Care Unit, PICU, air ambulance. As there would be no room for us, Susan and I decided to go to Edmonton on our own, ahead of time. Take-charge friends stepped in, drove us to the airport, bought tickets and waved us off. Then they returned to the hospital to pray with our eldest, 21 year old Seth, who had stayed with his little brother. Our friend Ann pinned a green scapular on John's remaining clothing. Within minutes, he began to crack jokes with Seth.

Hours later, John arrived at the PICU of the University Hospital, where we were waiting for him. Our concern about brain damage receded, only to be replaced with worry over the immense swelling of his throat and jaw. The medical staff kept him intubated for fear his throat would close. His head looked like a damaged porcupine.

The PICU is a place that God might have designed to make parents love their kids to insane lengths. For example, in the bed next to John lay a dot of a thing, a tiny three year old Korean girl who had been thrown through the windshield of the parents' car. The father and mother sat stock-still for two days staring at that motionless black-haired dot. Sometimes the father would pick her up and hold her in his lap. Suddenly, on the third day, when the father had her in his lap, she sat up and started babbling away as if nothing had happened. The father was silent, motionless for the first few minutes, but from across the room, you could feel him starting to relax from sheer joy. Eventually, he smiled.

John underwent surgery to reconstruct his jaw and lived on milkshakes for a month. We made a big fuss over him. Hitting the local papers and TV cheered him up considerably. We told him that his pain, and publicity, might save other kids' lives if they wore their helmets because of it.

You'd never know now that he had come within millimetres of death. The only physical sign is a tiny scar on his jaw line. He should not have recovered as fully and as speedily as he did – the power of prayer again. His behaviour isn't noticeably different either. He is still an uncommonly affectionate and giving son.

Susan and I, on the other had, continue to feel the impact. It's something to witness the uncanny bravery of small children. It's something to realise you could give up one of your children if God wanted it. It's something to realise concretely that the thing you have been given, the things you treasure in life, can be whisked away in a second. In our prayers, we knew we had no 'leverage' with God; we were talking, begging for unreasonable mercy. We had nothing else left, and came away thinking you don't need much else. Over the past year, we've all pondered what matters most to us.

Seth considers the priesthood, because of the accident and what surrounded it. Who knows, but it was a significant event in his life. I've quit a hectic job. If soul, family, then sustenance are our priorities, why was that third priority eating all my energy? We've considered moving, taking up a life based on our real treasures. Our family is bound together with a deepened love. We know God's mercy first hand.

Ten

Disaster, Rage and Repentance

by Michael O'Brien

Like many well-intentioned parents of our generation, my wife and I believed that child-rearing was largely a matter of finding the right method. Oh, we believed in prayer and grace well enough, and we knew there were variations in temperament that made some children a little more difficult to raise than others. But we were convinced that no child could resist the high octane mixture of our faith, our affection and our parenting skills.

Then the Lord gave us Ben; I will not belabour misdemeanours. Only let me say that from the moment of his birth he was an utterly delightful, exhausting, exasperating and fascinating phenomenon whom heaven decided to drop into our laps for the good of our souls. He was strong-willed, imaginative, utterly charming, very energetic and . . . and . . . .

Well, perhaps I could sum him up by saying that an elderly woman once came up to me in a doctor's waiting room and patted my arm, an arm that was busy wrestling with a wildly thrashing two-year old Ben. She gave me the sweetest smile, one that hinted at some secret joke.

'I know just how you feel', she said, 'I had a child like this. And I want you to know that they grow up to be the most wonderful people.'

That was some reassurance, because at the time my wife and I were only just coping from moment to moment. I spent a lot of time repairing broken objects and rescuing Ben from life-threatening predicaments. We were wracking our brains to figure out where we had gone wrong in the parenting recipe and were suffering that peculiar pain felt by those who have been secretly, oh-so-humbly, superior and were now living in the wreckage of their demolished theories. I badly needed a word of reassurance that day. I went home and told Sheila about it, and a light came back into her eyes. We repeated the lady's words to each other often. Very often.

I recall one ordinary Saturday especially. That morning, Ben's brothers and sisters had built him a large castle of wooden blocks. It had taken them half an hour to erect this fabulous creation, and it took Ben five seconds to demolish it. The older children rebuilt it for him only to see it destroyed once again. Over and over they repeated this game. We couldn't help laughing at Ben's delight as each time the walls came tumbling down. Perhaps we guessed that great things were being learned that day. The older ones were learning patience, of course. And Ben was learning something else at a very deep level, maybe the notion that even when we destroy things, they can be rebuilt again with a little help from our friends.

After lunch, Sheila went off grocery shopping with the older children, leaving me with Ben and seven year old Elizabeth. Now I have a confession to make. I am one of those time-harassed fathers who tend to bring work home – usually a big mistake. Because I am an artist and a writer, my work *is* at home, which further complicates the matter. I also tend to get distracted. And so, I try to keep the door to my studio firmly shut when the work day is over.

But on this particular afternoon, I was feeling unusually time-haunted and I was rushing. Sheila and I hadn't been sleeping too well either, because one of Ben's recurrent ear infections had flared up during the past few days. In addition, I was desperately trying to complete a painting commission in order to pay the bills. This desperation – 'quiet desperation' Thoreau called it – lurks at the edges of so many fathers' lives. Our world gets us galloping before we know it. We rush through our lives, trying to cram it all in, though no one has yet explained to me why we have to have it 'all'. And in order to have it all, a large number of people, including many Catholics, simply eliminate children from their lives in one way or another.

Now my wife and I have not eliminated children, but we were suffering the rushing syndrome and weren't coping with it too well. One of my coping devices was to cram in some work. And so on this deceptively quiet Saturday afternoon, while Ben and Elizabeth seemed occupied in the toy box, I ran upstairs to the studio and spread my painting boards onto the floor. It took me fifteen minutes to sand down the surfaces and to prepare the *gesso*, the liquid base layer that must be applied before the colour pigment. I was concentrating on all this, and had just begun to roll the first coat of white gesso onto several boards, when Elizabeth appeared at the doorway.

'Daddy, can we have a fire?' she said.

'What do you mean a fire, Lizzie?' I mumbled distractedly.

'I'm making a play house in the old stone fence that fell down, and I want to have a little fireplace in it'.

'Okay', I said, barely listening.

'Can I get some matches?' she added as she trotted away down the hall.

'Sure, okay', I said without thinking.

When the meaning of her last question penetrated, I called after her, 'No, Lizzie. No matches!'

I heard a little voice pipe up in reply, and assumed that she had heard me. I turned back to my work.

Twenty minutes later I was busily applying the second coat when Elizabeth burst in wild-eyed and cried, 'Dad, the field's on fire!'

'Oh no! Where's Ben?! He's in the house. He's okay. He didn't get burned'.

I stumbled down the stairs, crashed into a wall, careened out the kitchen door, and plunged into a nightmare. A small inferno raced off down the tinder-dry field, overgrown with thick, dead hay, from the direction of the stone fence. Perhaps I should mention that, first of all, burning fields at this time of year was illegal; secondly, the field was not ours; and thirdly, it was bordered by a stretch of very dry evergreen trees belonging to our neighbour.

I ran through the house, found a blanket and hurriedly soaked it with water in the kitchen sink. Then I bolted for the field, praying hard. Mercifully, the wind suddenly changed and began to blow the fire back toward its burnt-out core. That gave me a few precious minutes in which to race along the fire-line dragging the wet blanket. In the meantime Elizabeth had the good sense to uncoil the garden hose and turn it on. Working together we eventually extinguished the fire.

I heartily thanked God for the wind change. Panting for breath, covered with soot, aching from a few minor burns, soaked with black water, and suffering a few blown fuses in my nervous system, I lay down on the front lawn. At that moment my wife drove in with the groceries.

'What happened?' she asked.

'We had a little accident', I explained from the horizontal position.

'Oh, no! Was it Ben?'

'No', I said sombrely. 'It was Daddy'.

We laughed.

After the explanations and excuses and forgiveness and sympathy were concluded, Sheila said, 'Where's Ben?'

We both looked at each other and galloped for the house.

I knew there was a problem when I saw the little white footprints going up and down the stairs and along the hallway. I met him at the door of my studio. He was grinning at me in a mood of great delight.

'Puppa-guldy-guldy-paint-googly-ga! Paint!' he said.

'Oh, Ben', I sighed. 'What does guldy-guldy-googly-ga mean?'

But I already knew.

Sure enough, while I was fighting the fire, he had broken into the studio and had run barefoot back and forth across my partly dried boards. The footprints were embedded in the gesso, which was now thoroughly dry. It would all have to be sanded again and repainted. A half day's work lost! I controlled my irritation and gently led him to the bathroom.

I glanced at Sheila and forced out a laugh.

She went downstairs to the kitchen to clean that mess, while I plunked Ben into the bathtub and washed him down with the hose attached to our bathtub tap which functions as our shower. I started to clean myself up as best I could. Then the telephone rang, and I ran to answer it, leaving Ben splashing around with his toy boats in a shallow tub. If I were detained on the phone, I thought, Sheila would soon be back upstairs to oversee the drying off.

It was a long, long call. When I returned to the bathroom, I found Ben standing, holding the hose, staring at it as if mesmerised, and directing a steady blast of water onto the floor. In fact, an inch of water covered the floor, draining away down vents, joints and cracks to the room below.

Then it hit me – the room below! The room below was the dining room, and only three hours before I had sealed off that room. Within it I had left a large painting, its colours drying. It was too big to fit into any other room in the house and had to dry flat on its back. I had spread a plastic sheet on the floor, its edges curled up to form a kind of huge basin. Into this trough I had laid my painting.

I ran downstairs and unlocked the dining room. Inside I found the mural lying completely saturated, submerged in a pool of water leaked from the ceiling above. The subject of the painting, appropriately, was the baptism of the Lord. This time I did not laugh. The kind of board on which I paint must never be subjected to water, because the fibres separate, and the paint peels off. This piece of art had taken me six weeks to complete and Ben had wiped it out in one stroke. Not only was the painting destroyed but my vocation as a Christian artist was drowned forever, I thought.

Trying to survive as an artist with a large family, during a period which does not value art, let alone religious art, makes for a certain kind of tension. Financially, we are always living on the edge.

When you teeter constantly on the brink of disaster, life can feel like abandonment at times.

As I stared down at my ruined career, I felt a wave of utter frustration and rage. For the first time in my life I was tempted to strike a child in anger. I didn't. Instead I roared very angry, ugly words at him. Fortunately, he did not understand the words. He was totally dumbfounded by my reaction; after all, what's a little water between friends? But I saw his joyful eyes grow dark with fear and confusion under the storm of my anger. He hid from me in his mother's arms and cried deep sobs out of the bottom of his soul.

I had to do some reflection. This quiet little Saturday afternoon had offered me a moment of revelation – a quick glance into an unflattering mirror, the black waters of my own soul. 'What is the source of this rage?' I asked myself. 'Where on earth did it come from?'

In a moment of grace, I saw that right there at the bottom of my soul there was a radical lack of trust in God. No doubt it is a remnant of the Fall of Man, and yes, no doubt, most people bear the same scar in a variety of forms, but I had always assumed that it had no real power over me. I could never understand child-abusers, wife-abusers, or husband-abusers. Oh, I knew that every one has their bad days, their moments of temptation. But violence! Never! Even emotional violence is repugnant to me.

A good friend of ours once confessed with some shock in his voice that when his new born child came home from the hospital, and he and his wife were suffering their first experience of baby colic and the sleepless nights which accompany it, he had to fight back a mad impulse to throw the baby down the stairwell. The feeling came and went in a flash, but it shook him. I must hasten to assure the reader that this admission came from a sane, loving man, easily the most devoted father and husband I have ever met. Another outstanding parent, a woman so wise and kind that she deserves to be an icon of Catholic motherhood, once told me, in a tone of pained bewilderment, that she has at times felt like throwing her squalling infant through the picture window. These are ugly emotions, not the sort of thing one likes to admit, although they seem to be fairly common.

Now, here I was faced with the same nasty little impulse within *me*. I did not like it. I did not like what it was telling me about myself, and to compound the problem, I did not like that I did not like it, because this was a sure indication that pride was entwined with the original wound. Yes, I had prided myself on being a good father, imperfect of course, but devoted. And people had often told me that I'm a rather gentle fellow. So what was going on here? For the first time it hit me with a kind of unprecedented totality that I am like all my brothers and sisters, a member of that species known as fallen man. And I was seeing that, given the wrong set of circumstances, I could become capable of practically anything. This was not a pleasant discovery. This was not, as the pop-psychologists say, *self-affirming*.

No, I did not feel too good about myself at that moment. As a matter of fact, I did not like myself at that moment, and with good reason. Such incidents, if we will accept them, are a great grace. They are a testing. They offer a priceless moment of choice, the choice between growth or escape into deeper blindness, denial, hardness of heart and the blaming of everyone under the sun except one's self.

I stood there staring at Benjamin. He stared back, wondering what I would do next. The pool of lava within me was waiting to erupt, boiling with anger, paint, the suspicion that maybe nothing ultimately matters. The fear that all our efforts and sacrifices to create are eventually brought to nothing, destroyed by a whim in a meaningless universe. The fear that neither forgiveness nor hatred makes any difference. Was that the source of it? Or was it a feeling of being parachuted into a hostile century, heaped down with exhausting burdens in a landscape that seems to be growing darker by the day.

Men especially are afflicted to the depth of our beings with a sense of unacknowledged aloneness and fear. In this state we cannot bear to look into the gaping core of that wound. We dread to go down into the very centre of ourselves because we are afraid we might find there at the bottom: nothing. A trapdoor falling open into nothingness. If that were to happen, our aloneness would be not just personal abandonment in a dark place from which there is no escape. Is that the source? Is it because we think we are alone at the bottom of this deep, deep pit? And that pit is my very self?

Is it any wonder that most of us pursue the successful life with a kind of 'quiet desperation'? A comfortable life, kept well under control, can delay that moment of hard grace. After all, who wants pain? Moreover, what's wrong with a nice life? Well, nothing, as long as you don't pursue it at any cost. Nothing, as long as you don't try to preserve it by eliminating human beings. Nothing, as long as it remains within the limits of what is appropriate to the dignity of the human person. But be forewarned, a lifetime spent avoiding unpleasantness can deform us badly without our even knowing it. Unsuspecting, we can become incapable of sacrifice, and worse, incapable of hearing the truth.

Jesus says that the truth will set us free. He also says that it is harder for a rich man to enter the kingdom of heaven than for a camel to pass through the eye of a needle. A hard saying! There are many kinds of riches, and men who are materially poor are not exempt from them. I would maintain that the truth sets us free when we become willing to be poor to the core of our being. When we can look into the darkness, trusting that Jesus dwells there already, believing that there in the very centre of our fears, is not nothingness, but Love himself, waiting for us to meet him. To meet him *there*. *There* in the absolute poverty of our human state. Until then, until we begin to really learn to trust God, we will either continue to choose various means of escape, or we will slide slowly into a habit of bitterness. Either we begin to accept the innate poverty of the human condition, or we eventually fall victim to a spirit of rage and rebellion. If we refuse to learn this absolutely essential lesson, then quiet desperation can gradually become despair.

Trust is a choice. We cannot always help our feelings. But our will is our own. In exhaustion, desolation, darkness, sickness and doubts, we can choose to flee into the Lord's own arms. We must pray, and we must make a conscious decision to pray, especially in those times when we *least* feel like praying. We can make mental acts of trust in divine providence, especially when our surroundings are shambles. When temptation pounds away at our hearts, we can run to the Lord in the sacraments, hide ourselves in his Sacred Heart, cry out to him from beneath the cross. We will find that he always supplies the grace necessary for bearing our crosses. Step by step, little by little, we learn that God is infinitely patient, and generous, with those who sincerely seek him. The fight against fear may even be a life-long effort, but still we mustn't be unduly fearful. Where else but in fearful situations will we learn courage? Where but in disaster zones will we learn to trust absolutely?

All of this came to me in those seconds while Ben and I stood staring at each other across the ruins of our life. Then, I went down on my knees and held out my arms to him. He ran over and whispered, 'Sorry, Papa!' And I told him through the language of hands and poverty-stricken words just how sorry I was too. He hugged me hard. I hugged him back. Then together we got out rags, mops and towels, and worked side by side to clean up the disaster. I noted Ben's special eagerness to help. I especially noted an odd little smile on his face. And it made me think.

Every one of our acts sends shock-waves into the world and into the lives of others. Like this naive two-year-old, we often do not grasp the results of our destructive choices, or our omissions. We think we aren't hurting anyone. Yet, the effects are there, invisible but powerful. Sin is the damage done to 'God's work of art', as Saint Paul calls us. Each of us is made in the image and likeness of God, and every sin, or failure to choose good, defaces that image, an image that cost a great deal to make and a great deal to ransom. Abortion, for example, destroys a whole human person and severely damages the mother. A contraceptive mentality denies that the Father-Creator made us properly, and exhibits a deep fear and disbelief in divine providence. 'A little white lie' or a true fact repeated as gossip, even 'pious' gossip, can set off lines of falling dominoes, destroying relationships, ruining communities. A father's rage and resentment, unrepented, can prevent a child from growing into the whole loving person he was intended to become.

At some point the billions of tragic chain reactions must have an end. When Jesus died in our place on the Cross, he made it possible for us to be freed from the tyranny of our destructive impulses. We need no longer be slaves to sin. If we do fall, we can simply run to our Father and say we are sorry. The Father's power is then liberated in our hearts to rebuild things once again. God, in his tender love for humanity understands us very well. He refuses to spoil us. He is not some cosmic nagging parent who eternally follows his children about, complaining and picking up after them. No, he is a truly loving Father, who respects us so much that he demands that we grow. He desires to heal and to teach us in order that we might become free, capable of love and truth.

I was astonished at how cheerfully Benjamin went about mopping up my painting. I was even more surprised at how working together with him restored my own spirits. Later that day, we went for a walk in woods, alone together, up the hill across from our place. I put Ben on my shoulders and he chattered happily, holding tight to my forehead. We talked of many things, he and I. Not all of it was intelligible, in fact hardly any of it. But some words that are beyond the need for language, and maybe they are the most important words of all.

That day, I think Ben learned that no matter how much chaos he caused, he was forgiven and loved. He learned that his father would help him restore the creation he had damaged. He learned that his father desired to be with him. The language of my shoulder and hands told him that I was *with* him. He was safe. At one point, I put him up into the branches of a tree that was just budding new leaves. It had been a long, bitter winter, and it was just recently past. The tree was a cottonwood which around here we call the 'balm of Gilead'. Its buds are coated with a sticky resin that smells sweeter than incense. Ben sniffed it and grinned. Then, he leapt from the branch and landed in my arms.

'What trust!' I thought, 'Maybe someday I'll learn to do that with God!'

We walked on, babbling about leaves and squirrels. The sunshine was healing. The birds were singing, trusting, just being. It was an ordinary moment. Nothing cosmic. Nothing that he would remember on the conscious level, but something so strong that I suspect it penetrated to the hidden places of his soul.

Ben is almost eight years old now. He is the delight of our hearts. He is an irrepressible, joyous, imaginative boy, full of energy, silly jokes and faith. He makes wood-block castles for his little sister, writes and illustrates home-made books for her, though admittedly they are full of trucks and tigers and swords, longs for his First Communion, reminds us to have daily prayer time whenever we are absent-minded, reads, rides a bicycle, dances, recites poetry, ties his shoelaces and is struggling with the intricacies of telling time from a clock.

In the months following our disaster, as I awaited the inevitable deterioration of the painting, I thought a great deal about that smile on Ben's face. And I wondered if maybe on the hidden face of God there is another smile, hinting at a secret joke. The impossible happened: the painting simply refused to crumble. Not a fibre was out of place. Almost six years later it remains in perfect condition, thanks be to God!

Eleven

Mary Helen

by Robert Otrembiak

Call me crazy if you don't believe me, but we are witnesses to a miracle! Now that most, if not all of the facts are in, I'll fill you in on the best news I've ever received in my life.

Our dear and sweet Mary Helen, although she is the joy of our lives, does not like to sleep. Only a few months old, she has difficulty digesting even mother's milk and so spends many hours in intestinal discomfort. A couple of weeks ago, her agitation increased greatly. She developed a fever and began vomiting whenever we fed her. The doctor ordered a sonogram of her stomach to look for a stomach disorder. Jenn and I wish it could have been that simple.

The sonogram showed lesions on Mary Helen's liver. Our paediatrician was in no position to diagnose these lesions based solely on the ultrasound, so he arranged for Mary Helen to be admitted to Hershey Medical Center, the finest hospital for paediatric cancer treatment in the mid-Atlantic region. A CAT-scan indicated that the lesions were tumours. The scan also found a large tumour behind the liver near the spine. Our oncologist surmised that Mary Helen had a neuroblastoma, a tumour that leads to bone marrow and bone tissue cancer. She was released from the hospital for the weekend but scheduled to return the following week for a bone scan.

The bone scan revealed strange shadows on Mary Helen's right wrist and left ankle bones. The doctors said it could be cancer in the bone tissue, which is much more serious than if it had been only in the marrow. They admitted her immediately and scheduled a biopsy.

All the while, little Mary Helen handled the situation as well as any six-week old could. She was confused and frustrated when denied her parents and nourishment. Jennifer and I could only hope and pray that some good would come from the hell she was experiencing. I still feel a pang in my heart when I recall the look of, 'Why won't you help me?' on Mary Helen's face, after she'd been denied feedings for twelve hours before surgery.

I felt sorrow unlike any I had ever known as I handed my baby daughter to the surgeons who would perform the operation. Five hours later, the head surgeon met with us to tell us what had transpired. They had inserted a permanent catheter-I.V. down Mary Helen's throat and out her chest. By tapping this plug, the doctors drew blood, gave medication and chemotherapy. Inserting the tube left an inch-long scar on her neck. During the operation, the doctors also took samples of the liver tumours for analysis. However, when the surgeon reached behind her liver to inspect the tumour near her spine he couldn't find it.

He had a spur-of-the moment meeting with the radiologist and the other concerned physicians. There was no denying that a tumour appeared on the CAT-scan, yet he had found nothing. He tripled the size of the incision, clamped open the flesh, and did a step-by-step inspection of the area. He located everything shown on the scan except the tumour! It was gone! Was it ever there? A resident doctor and the nurses all agreed that they had seen misleading X-rays, but never a deceptive CAT-scan. We definitely had a mystery on our hands. The doctors were stunned.

For us, the news that affirmed these events as miraculous came two days later, when our doctor reported that the tumours on the liver were benign, and probably would heal themselves. That meant no long hospital stays, no chemotherapy and no bone marrow transplants! In addition, Mary Helen recovered so well that they sent her home that weekend. She will be returning to the clinic as an outpatient regularly just to verify that all is well. It appears that she has colic, and the continual vomiting was nothing more than a virus.

What an adventure we had. We are convinced that nothing short of divine intervention caused that tumour to disappear. For whatever reason, the Lord was pleased to test Jennifer and I. Countless people, most of whom we don't know and will never meet, prayed diligently for Mary Helen, and we believe that the Lord answered our prayers. Since it can't be proven, this event truly is a matter of faith. It's not as if the doctor *saw* the tumour during one procedure only to have it disappear before the next. But Jennifer and I always will believe that God has touched our lives personally through our little Miracle Baby.

Twelve

Forgiveness, Stars, and Saint God

by Petroc Willey

I am getting used to the idea that God wants to speak to me and teach me through our young daughter. Now this isn't a case like Balaam's Ass, because Charis certainly can speak. She's three years old and has been chattering happily for quite a while. But she is at that age where much of what she says is a little like speaking in tongues, because her words can carry more weight than she realises. She is at that refreshing and frightening stage where directness and honest-speaking have not yet been tempered and refined by polite convention. What she says comes straight from the heart, and her words can chill you to the marrow, just like the Word of God.

I shouldn't find it surprising that God uses Charis as a vehicle for teaching me. Vatican II, turning the way we normally think about parents and teachers upside down, said that children 'greatly contribute to the good of their parents' (*Gaudium et Spes,* paragraph 50). As a parent, I tend to imagine that the bottom line of our relationship is my doing *her* good, but I am growing used to the idea that it is really – as our wise Mother the Church teaches us – the other way around.

Now I want to assure you that Charis is not any sort of child prodigy. She is just an ordinary, extraordinary daughter, like anyone's daughter. At the same time, her very first word should have alerted me to the theological benefits I was going to receive from her. Her first word was 'Abba'.

Since that moment I have realised that when Jesus gave us 'Abba' as the name for His Father He was giving us the first word which *He* spoke. And it is the most basic word for *us* too: the first recognisable word uttered by us is this word of trust and communion.

The Catechism of the Catholic Church has a sentence near the very beginning, where it teaches that there is an invitation for Man to converse with God *'as soon as he comes into being'* (paragraph 27). And so there was Charis, speaking with her Creator, her Abba, a beautiful daughter of God. Only then did she turn and speak with us, her parents. Like Jesus, Charis went instinctively to her Father's House and was found there by her parents, communing with her Abba in secret. For a brief moment, Katherine and I saw with the certainty of a sudden revelation that we were *pro*-creators. And with this realisation came a levelling of all our relationships – we appreciated what an amazing equality we remind children that they share with their parents as we all together say the 'Our Father'. Yes, Charis, I'm your Daddy, but we both have the same Abba, and we are both eternally children.

That was her first word. She is now almost three. In the past few months she has uttered three mighty words of prophecy, and I have only myself to blame if I don't benefit from them. The first was a word of forgiveness; the second, a word of hope; and the third was a word of love. Coming in Advent, they prepared me well for the Feast of Christmas.

The first, then, was a word of forgiveness. This Word of the Lord was given early on a wintry evening as I was driving out to fill our car with petrol. Charis was in the back seat, in her child's chair. Suddenly, and without warning, a car shot out of a side-road in front of me. I slammed on the brakes and narrowly avoided hitting it. Meanwhile, the other car had gone roaring down the road, its tail-lights now flickering in the distance. I was indignant, and the indignation rapidly turned to fury, my blood racing in my veins. That car was travelling far too fast in a built-up area. I would avenge myself – and my daughter. We might have been killed. My car became a steed as it leaped down the road in pursuit. I was overtaken by a technological frenzy. I was Law and Order, pursuing a Vehicle of Unrighteousness. And now all that mattered was that I was gaining ground, and the distance between us was lessening.

Then, out of the darkness behind me and out of the silence – for my fury was wordless and expressed only in acceleration – came a word: 'He didn't mean to, Daddy'.

Somehow I knew that was from God and meant for me and it broke the spell of madness. I relaxed and slowed down. 'Abba, Daddy, they don't mean to', Jesus said on the Cross. 'Forgive them. Let them roar off into the distance. Don't pursue them with your vengeance. They don't know what they are doing.' Jesus' last words about us were words of forgiveness at our blindness, our not seeing what we do as we crash blindly through His creation.

The second Word I received from the Lord that Advent was the most mysterious, and I record it not because I fully understand its meaning, but because it moved me deeply. It came as a word of hope.

It was given a few weeks later, about the middle of Advent. Once again I was driving, with Charis in the back of the car. It was dark, a beautiful star-filled night. Then Charis spoke.

'Daddy, we mustn't touch the sun. That would burn us.'

'Yes, it would.' I was glad to think that she was a girl with good basic sense.

'We mustn't touch the moon either.' She spoke anxiously. 'That would burn us as well.'

'I see.' I tried to sound affirming, but non-committal. Maybe she knew something I didn't, but I wasn't so sure about that one.

Then, full of happiness, with all anxiety gone, 'But the *stars* won't burn us. We can touch the stars.'

Something about stars made me think of all the hopes I had for our marriage and family. Over the years these hopes had been so often damaged and undermined by my pettiness, self-sufficiency and pride. They had become like distant stars – brilliant, gleaming, but far away, inaccessible. I realised that, following the inevitable disappointments and light friction of daily family living, I had uneasily come to terms with what I told myself it was 'realistic' to expect from our marriage. In reality, though, I had simply dismissed that beautiful, but painful messenger, hope. I had cut the coat of my expectations to fit my own diminished reality, and called it 'being sensible'

But now it was as if the stars came down from the night sky and settled themselves around the car, accessible, friendly. Suddenly, my hopes could be touched again. I knew that God was not content with the half-satisfaction I was busy accustoming myself to. God wanted to fulfil every hope I had for our marriage – and in ways deeper and more enduring that I could possibly imagine. Like shining angels, our stars *could* be touched and we would not be burned.

The third and last Word was a Word of love. It was Christmas Eve. Charis was very excited. Every decoration had been handled with immense care and placed tenderly on the tree. Every wooden bird and flying angel, trumpet at the ready, had been made comfortable on one of the branches. Now we were settling down and getting a small sack ready for Santa.

Katherine and I were concerned that Charis should be able to move naturally from a belief in Father Christmas, not to unbelief and a dismissal of mystery but, as the years passed, to a sense of a greater, more awe-inspiring mystery, of which Father Christmas is just a pale shadow. And so we had decided to call him 'Santa Claus' – an easier transition to 'Santa Nicholas'.

After a short discussion about Santa's possible mode of entry into a flat like ours which lacked the necessary chimney, I confided to her – one grown-up speaking to another – 'Of course, Charis, Santa is *really* Saint Nicholas.' I thought that I may as well begin the process now. Charis was busy eating a yoghurt. She looked up conspiratorially and whispered back, 'Daddy, it's *really* Saint God, isn't it?'

There, in one sentence, on a single evening, she made the leap which Katherine and I had been patiently rehearsing to ourselves and planning as something that might take place over the next five or so years. And we had been thinking only of explaining the mystery of how the brightly wrapped presents would arrive under the Christmas tree. Charis had reminded me of the real present – Saint God Himself, the Present and the Giver all rolled into one. That is what we were really celebrating.

Speak, Lord, Your servant is listening.

Thirteen

I Buried Jesus, Mum

by Maria Delft

A dull winter's day. The first snowflakes of the year. A look at the kitchen clock told me that I had been staring out of the window, hypnotised by that steady falling and twirling of white stars, for an hour. But it temporarily relieved the ache in my heart.

'Mum, can I play outside?' yelled Luke, who had just bounced in the back door from school. 'And can I take the toboggan to the hill?'

I looked at our nine year old, that beaming face, his cheeks all apple-red from the cold.

'Okay, Luke, for an hour, but I want you home by five. You said you'd help Dad set up the Christmas tree. Don't make him wait for you.'

Luke agreed to everything and anything as long as he could get outside. Off he went.

'That Christmas tree', I grumbled, 'It's only done for Luke'.

For ourselves there was no purpose anymore, especially this year. I just wasn't in the mood. The problems in our marriage had increased during the past few months, and I couldn't resolve them. I took care of the home. Pete was the bread winner. Plain and simple, cut and dried! No problem, really . . . except that the atmosphere in the house was stifling, and the Christmas season wouldn't change any of it.

Christmas would probably make it worse. Friday was grocery shopping night. After arriving home from work, Pete usually went out to do that chore. I quickly made up a list, otherwise, he would accuse me of indecision. Then I heard the door slam. He had come home earlier than I expected.

'Any mail?' he said, looking at me.

'Only some Christmas cards'.

'That can wait. Is Luke home?'

'Yes . . . er, no . . . I mean I didn't know you'd be home so early. He's off playing with friends in the snow. He won't be long'.

No sooner had I said the words than Luke came in, screaming, 'Those kids down the street ploughed into us with their toboggan and I crashed'.

Pete put an exploratory hand on Luke's hip where the source of discomfort seemed to be.

'Do you feel that?'

Luke produced a tormented look, but a remark from Dad worked wonders, 'Son, if the pain's that bad I might have to do the Christmas tree and the crib all alone'.

Luke had been looking forward to this for weeks. Decorating the tree with lights, the glittering balls, angels' hair and whatever odds and ends we could find. Then the home-made strings of popcorn. The tin-foil icicles he'd made long ago in kindergarten, carefully preserved in a box through the year. The tiny antique brass musical instruments handed down from my side of the family, the lovely straw starts and crosses from Pete's ancestors. Luke especially liked to help his dad erect the stand for the crib and cover it with bark or moss.

'It doesn't hurt so bad now, Dad. I can do it. Can we start right away?'

I felt some of my sadness lift as I watched them. Pete and Luke worked in good spirits, Luke with vast enjoyment. His dad had great ideas, hiding the little light in the back stable behind the ox for effect. Leaving Luke and Pete to busy themselves, I went upstairs to do some ironing.

Suddenly, Pete had an idea. 'Luke, you keep working on the crib till it's finished and I'll drive over to the hamburger stand.

Then Mum won't have to cook and we'll soon be on our way to shopping.'

Luke especially liked the novelty of permission to work all alone on the tree and the crib. 'Come here you little donkey', he said. 'I'm going to place you first. They say you're the dumb one. Nothing doing, when you're in the stable with Jesus, you're not that dumb.'

From upstairs I could hear him chattering, but supposed he was still talking with his dad. When I came down I saw that Pete was not there and simply concluded that he had gone out to the garage for replacement bulbs or an extension cord. I watched Luke gather the little porcelain animals all around Mary and Joseph. He was very careful because he knew from experience that the old figures were fragile. He was so absorbed in his work that he did not realise Mum stood behind him. I enjoyed the loving scene for a few moments then went to the kitchen to prepare supper.

Shortly after, Pete returned. He arrived in the kitchen with that look on his face which I used to love; it was full of secret delight in a surprise he had for me. He thought he was saving me the trouble of making supper.

'Why didn't you check with me first?' I snapped. 'That would have been a more useful act of love.' I knew that on the practical level I was right, of course. But I couldn't understand why I was being so nasty about his little thoughtful thoughtlessness.

'Couldn't you have told me?' I said coldly, louder than necessary. 'Now we're stuck with a double meal. And you're always complaining about left-overs!'

'Don't make such a fuss, Maria', he said quietly.

Looking back now, I suspect that Luke often heard arguments such as this, after he was in bed. But this was the first incident of open warfare.

'I only wanted to surprise you. You're so uptight', Pete went on.

Before we knew it our voices were raised. Dad's fist hit the table in frustration and despair. Mum rushed past Luke, crying, ran upstairs and slammed the bedroom door.

'Merry Christmas, Merry Christmas', I sobbed into my pillow.

Downstairs, Pete slammed the back door shut behind him.

There was dead silence.

Luke sat beneath the tree listening to the empty house. He looked at the infant Jesus in his hands. He was frightened, because at school he heard a lot about parents who had separated or were getting divorced. Half the kids in his class no longer had a Mum or Dad living at home. Several more had never had more than one parent.

Tears came to his eyes as he rose and headed towards the stairs, hoping to find Mum. But he stumbled over boxes and dropped the Christ child. Horrified, he rebuked himself, what now? Suddenly, he had an idea. He would bury Jesus in the garden. Nobody need ever find out. Jesus was simply lost.

Luke had quite a job chopping out a hole in the garden's frozen black soil in the dark. He used his scout hatchet and one of my kitchen knives. The broken shards of porcelain gashed his hands as he dug, terrified that his crime would be discovered, for these exquisitely formed, painted figurines were a family heirloom, more than a hundred years old.

When Jesus was buried, Luke felt very alone and empty inside. He went upstairs to the bathroom, bandaged his hand with some difficulty, then tapped on my door calling, 'Mum, Mum . . . ' in a small frightened voice. Hurt, angry, consumed with self-pity and upset over why I didn't know what was wrong with me, I ignored his knocking. 'Serve, serve, serve', I growled to myself, 'is that all I'm good for!' I decided that Luke could just go away and Pete could darn well look after him. I hoped they enjoyed their hamburgers. Good luck to them.

After awhile, the tapping stopped and Luke tiptoed downstairs. He returned to the living room, turned on the television and sat staring at it, seeing nothing.

At midnight Pete came home to find Luke sound asleep on the couch. Pete turned off the set, picked the boy up and carried him to bed without waking him. Next morning, and for the next three days, a stifling silence prevailed in our home. Luke endeavoured to help wherever possible, even eating his least favourite foods without complaint. Pete and I were both very kind to him, even though we studiously avoided each other.

While we had discovered the Christ child missing from the crib, we couldn't generate any emotion other than dull sadness. We did not question Luke as we normally would have. His crime remained undiscovered, and he felt guiltier than ever.

Still, Luke could not entirely repress his joy at the approach of Christmas, now only a day away. He had seen the crib in the church when his class went there to practise their flutes for the music at Midnight Mass. Luke longed for this celebration and his desperate pleas that we go as a family finally provoked a conversation between Mum and Dad. Reluctantly, Pete and I agreed to go.

Although we knew we were both at fault, Pete's faults loomed very large in my mind. He had gradually evolved into a workaholic to give Luke and I the 'best' things of life. His mind was always elsewhere. His moments of considerateness were sporadic and sometimes thoughtless. Recently he had started working on Sundays in order to supplement our income.

A few years back, after a little wrestling match with our consciences, we started using artificial contraception in order to avoid any complications in our already overstressed lives. One child was enough, we believed at the time, and now this belief seemed truer than ever. Yet I'd always wanted a large family, and so had Pete.

I loved Pete in the beginning. I asked myself in those early years how anyone could ever fall out of love the way we loved each other. But all that was gone now. After a while I couldn't pray in the old way and gradually let devotion after devotion go by the way side. Then I stopped praying altogether. Pete did too. Nevertheless, we had decided to send Luke to a Catholic school because we wanted a good foundation, an ethical belief-system, for him. Not that we wanted him to become like we had been in our youth, you know, *fanatical*. Yes, both Pete and I had outgrown the fanaticism, though for some reason we hadn't experienced much happiness in our new-found 'freedom'.

On my part, I had indulged in a habit of wallowing in resentments and punishing my husband for failing to be what I thought he should be, for not seeing me, not hearing me. I was sure he didn't love me anymore, and maybe, to tell you the truth, he didn't. I didn't like the person I was becoming.

Worst of all, we both stubbornly refused to give in and ask forgiveness. We were each convinced that the other should make the effort to seek forgiveness first. We'd stopped going to Mass a few months back. It all seemed so pointless. So much of what the Church taught just didn't make sense to our lives any more. Why for example, should two perfectly unhappy people stay chained to each other forever? 'Maybe our marriage is dead', I thought, 'in the same way that people die, maybe relationships die too'. It was an idea I was hearing more and more these days, repeated by independent, successful, formerly-married people who seemed quite happy chasing after careers and new 'relationships'.

Over the supper table on Christmas Eve, Pete and I looked at Luke's sparkling eyes.

'Please, Mum. Please, Dad. Can you come to Midnight Mass and hear me play?'

It was genuine begging. Who could resist that tone in his voice?

And so we went – for the sake of Luke. We entered the crowded church, uneasy for several reasons. All of it, the decorations, lights, children, atmosphere, was beautiful, but the beauty seemed to deepen my pain. For a moment, I thrilled to Luke's solo on his little brass flute, but I could not keep my mind on the festivities. Oh, God, how I loved him.

Then Pete, sitting stiffly beside me, took my hand gently and held it. What could I do? Tear my hand away while Luke was playing that heart-rending piece? So I enjoyed the comfort of allowing my hand to be held. Suddenly, I felt a drop of scalding water. I glanced down, astonished to see that this tear had come from Pete's eyes. He looked straight at me. The ache, the hardness, in me melted, spilling out of my eyes.

'Buried', was the word I heard.

We shook ourselves awake. Had so many minutes passed? Was that the priest speaking his homily from the pulpit?

'In the final analysis', he proclaimed, 'Jesus came on earth to die and to be buried. But his message of forgiveness does not allow a burial to be the final word. The final word is resurrection.'

After Mass, Pete took my hand again, gently, not forcing me. Again I allowed my hand to be taken.

He led me over to the crèche beside the tabernacle, and we knelt down together. We hadn't prayed in a long time. We knelt for what seemed forever, a quiet peaceful forever with no words. In a strange way, none and yet all of our problems had been solved.

Just then, Luke crashed into us, having been released from the choir. He knelt down between us, and as a family we gazed at the baby Jesus in the manger.

'Mum, Dad', he whispered, 'I buried Jesus'.

All at once I understood my boy's little crime. And I recognised my big one, the way for many years I too had been 'burying Jesus'. When was it I had stopped loving first? When was it I had stopped asking God for the grace to love? When had Pete stopped?

'No, no, no, Maria', I ordered myself. 'For just one moment, let's not talk about Pete and all his faults! Me! What about me?'.

When had I done it? When was it? When had I started nursing bitterness like a rotten candy in my mouth? Had Jesus not disappeared? What had happened to my soul?

As soon as we arrived home, Pete noticed a profound change in me. I gave him a big hug, thanked him, and told him I loved him. He asked forgiveness for not showing his love for me. I asked his forgiveness too, right there under the tree, with Luke listening – a beaming Luke.

What happened next, our son has never forgotten. He retold the story every Christmas thereafter, and in later years shared the tale with his younger brothers and sisters.

I lifted the crucifix from the wall and placed it carefully where the Christ child should have been in the manger.

'Jesus isn't buried', I said in a gentle voice, rubbing my hand through Luke's hair.

'Jesus lives . . . .'

Fourteen

Not Your Will, But Mine

by Astrid Nordholt

The Second Vatican Council was convened the summer before John and I were married, and we were ripe for the freedom it offered us. We were quick to open our windows and let the wind of the Holy Spirit blow into our buildings. The renewal of our faith began, continuing through many incidences of God in our lives, people we met, places we went, our involvements in the Church, books and articles we read.

Humanae Vitae was promulgated five years after our marriage, and, like many good Catholics, we chose to ignore it. The messages we were hearing were unclear, and, instead of studying it for ourselves, we believed what we read in the secular press and heard – or didn't hear – from the pulpit and in private. In those early years of the sixties, 'the pill' was new, and 'freedom of conscience' was the popular phrase. What we didn't know wouldn't hurt us, or would it? The fact that we had never read *Humanae Vitae* was not a factor; we believed as we heard from so many sources at the time that the document was not infallible, so why waste our time? Besides, we weren't into reading encyclicals! They were meant, we believed, for bishops and priests, who would then teach the people if they contained a message worth teaching. Accordingly, we adopted, and grew quickly in the 'contraceptive mentality' that began in the early 1960s.

Our attempts at contraception included 'the pill', the IUD and eventually the ultimate, definitive sterilisation, on our doctor's orders and the misguided advice of a wonderful priest. We thought we had the right to limit our family as we chose, by using whatever means were at our disposal. It was as if we were saying to God, 'Not your will, but mine be done'. Because of my strong Catholic upbringing I did have some misgivings, but put those aside in the desire to do what seemed to be prudent and right.

In spite of our efforts to arrange our lives and our family according to our own design, God gave us six beautiful and well-loved children. Still, we failed to listen to what God was saying to us, and to learn from the love he was showing us in each of those beautiful new lives.

He waited twenty-five years of marriage before confronting us with our sin.

Seven years before, when our children ranged in age from five to seventeen, we made a family retreat, which had the effect of drawing us closer to the Church and her teachings, and closer to each other as a family. Each year every member of the family looked forward to that time away; some summers we were blessed with the opportunity of making two retreats, and took many retreat weekends as well. We began wholeheartedly to embrace, one at a time, those aspects of Church life which we had rejected in our smorgasbord approach to our faith. The last of these was *Humanae Vitae*.

During several of those retreats and many private visits to our friends who are involved in family ministry, the subject of *Humanae Vitae* would be raised in various ways, either directly or by their sharing with us the burdens they were seeing couples carry because of contraception or direct sterilisation. We continued to ignore what they were saying, considering it to be our own business, a private matter between the two of us. Besides, it didn't apply to *us*, we reasoned, because we had always felt peaceful about our sterilisation. We truly believed it was God's will for us; our priest, whom we trusted to guide us in the right direction, had said it was right; with six children we had been generous enough, and surely that was all God expected of us!

We were sincere, but wrong.

We never shared our story with our friends, and became increasingly annoyed, uncomfortable and closed whenever the subject of sterilisation was mentioned. Even so, God kept moving us to return for more; we should have recognised him at work in the words of our friends and in our increasing uneasiness.

Gradually our hearts softened, and we began to talk about it with each other, examining our motives and actions in the light of what we had by this time learned about *Humanae Vitae* and other teachings of the Church. We were beginning to see our blatant disobedience, which could no longer be hidden behind the excuse of ignorance or 'freedom of conscience'; and we were beginning to realise that in affirming the peace we claimed we felt, we were actually denying the guilt.

Our wonderful priest, whom we love dearly, had been our authority; we had acted on his trusted word to us, a word which was improperly informed and wrong. However, we cannot transfer the blame for our actions because ultimately we had failed in *our* responsibility to seek the truth and to properly inform our own consciences. Father may have been our guide and mentor, but we were totally wrong in ignoring our own responsibility by relying on someone else to be our conscience.

In 1988, when we booked for another summer retreat, we somehow knew that the subject of our sterilisation was the big one we would be dealing with, and we were willing, and even eager to do so. It seemed that it was the last hurdle to our entering completely and unconditionally into the life of Christ and his Church. We knew this issue could no longer be buried if we were to be completely open to God's grace and will in our lives. By this time, living fully the life of God was what we wanted more than anything.

We arrived for our retreat eager and expectant, knowing that God would deal with us to the extent we were willing to give him permission to act and to accomplish his cleansing, healing and forgiveness. He had other plans. Two days after our arrival, we were called home because my father, who had been ill for some time, was in a coma and dying. With heavy hearts we began the six hour trip home, all of us bitterly disappointed that our week had evaporated, not to mention, of course, our concern for Dad . . . would we make it in time to see him alive? What would we find on our return home?

Over the next few days, as he rallied and seemed to recover, we couldn't help wondering what God had in mind, bringing us so close, only to shut the door. Dad died that Friday, and in the busyness of the funeral and burial there wasn't much time to think about sterilisation or retreats. However, God really did have another, more wonderful plan. The day after Dad had been buried, the director of the retreat house called to say there had been a cancellation for the following week; it was too late to fill it from the waiting list; we would be welcome if we felt up to it.

I remember feeling very raw and vulnerable as the retreat began, and indeed for most of the week I listened to the talks in something of a daze. I kept much to myself, seeking quiet and solitude, and found that I was completely unable to share in the conferences. As I spoke with other people in the occasional encounter, I felt like another person, an onlooker outside of myself. God had me where he wanted me; supple, vulnerable, out of my own control.

Early in the week we shared with the directors what was in our hearts, what had been churning all those years during all those visits when we refused to face our sin, what we now wanted to come to terms with and turn over to the Lord for his mercy. Their love and acceptance, gentleness and compassion prepared us for the sacrament of reconciliation the next day.

Our time of repentance was one of those mountains of God's grace, as we felt his great mercy and love wash over us and cleanse us completely. The sacrament was a truly powerful encounter with Christ; God was tangibly present, and Jesus stood with us in the person of the retreat priest, who led us, without judgement and with love, through each event and time in our marriage that needed to be brought into the light of God's forgiveness. God used him even to bring forth areas of sin that had been forgotten but never confessed. It was a time of knowing with certainty God's love and mercy, that he can and will forgive anything we have done and allow us to begin again with a new infilling of grace.

It was a time of looking back of course, as all great turning points in life are. For the first time we were able to see clearly some of the things that had happened to our relationships. We had not realised that, by being closed to new life, we were also closed to the life that existed, and had in some mysterious way cut the lines of communication with the six children we had, not to mention with each other.

Throughout our marriage, our attempts at contraception had been somewhat schizoid, one part of us saying 'no' to new life, the other wanting to trust God to provide. All along the way he had offered his hand to us, and we usually failed to see it or refused to take it. When we conceived, we blamed the method which 'obviously didn't work'. It did occur to us, however, that God had ordained we should have another child, no matter the means we were using to try to prevent it. We were grateful and joyful.

After we had come into a relationship with Jesus, fairly early in our marriage, when we had four children, we prayed together often, even in the act of love and felt profoundly the presence of God with us. After we were sterilised, we stopped praying in this way, not realising it until we looked back. It was not conscious; it just happened. We seemed to have shut God out of this part of our life and were unable or unwilling to recognise his presence and his desire to be part of what we were doing. We were like Adam and Eve in the garden, hiding from God after they had sinned. Cut off from each other, our communication began to suffer.

God continued to reach out to us, and we experienced early in this period a Marriage Encounter weekend. It was a great gift; the blessings were abundant and powerful, and for a time the fruit was oh, so sweet. However, it was not long before that experience died, again unnoticed until we looked back. It was like the seed planted on rock, which blooms beautifully at first, but shortly dies because the roots are shallow. The roots from our Marriage Encounter had nowhere to go beyond the surface of our relationship.

The trauma of sterilisation in our lives occurred just at the time that our family was beginning to enter the teen years. Again, in hindsight, we can see that it was the root of the difficulty we had relating with our children as they grew. Because of the presence of sin in our lives, we could not talk to them about virtue, about chastity, about morality. Although we desperately wanted to have clear communication with them, we caught ourselves constantly shutting them out, closing the door, lacking in compassion. The truth was important to us, even though we were living a lie, and we wanted to teach truth to our children, but we did it without love, because love was gone out of our lives.

When they were small, we used to have a great deal of fun with the children, and insignificant events were opportunities to laugh and play and enjoy each other. Winter picnics, table-top crafts, visits to horse stables and picking berries were all family fun events. After sterilisation, these times of joy ceased. We still had fun, but it was different; usually it was with other families, and less spontaneous. Our fun was more ordered, more planned and more directed. Life became much too serious. These observations are again in retrospect; we were not in any way aware of our sin, and yet subconsciously we were very *aware*.

Again we can see the hand of God reaching out to us, the mantle of our Lady protecting us, because in spite of it all, we are very close to our children, and they to us and to each other. In spite of us, God wove a bond that cannot be broken; he fashioned a family that in our brokenness we were unable to make, built relationships that in our poverty we could not build.

The ensuing weeks, months and years have been a grace-filled time of rebuilding. It has been and continues to be a struggle, one which at times we'd rather not face, but gradually results are beginning to show. We are building those bridges that were broken so many years ago, and we are strengthening the family bonds and relationships that God kept intact for us until we were able to do it ourselves with his help.

We have taken no steps towards reversing the sterilisation;

in our late forties, it seemed a further violation of the body to undergo reversal surgery, and redundant to learn about Natural Family Planning. In the ensuing years, however, we have in fact learned much about NFP and its wonderful benefits for marriage and family life. We do recognise, of course, the need to make reparation for the wrong we have done.

And so we have adopted and embrace monthly abstinence. We never dreamed that through abstinence we could grow in our love for one another, that we could actually deepen our relationship and become truly great friends and lovers. Each of us has a new appreciation of the other, a new understanding, a new respect, a new love. The experience has been like falling in love all over again. We always thought we had the best possible marriage, never realising how we were cheating ourselves and our children. God in his mercy has offered us the opportunity to repair and rebuild, and we are grateful. We have grown closer than we ever thought possible, sharing a new and beautiful intimacy.

Part of the pain we feel is that of having missed so much for those twelve years of 'elective infertility', and this pain continues to intensify as we learn more about Natural Family Planning. Doors have opened to us which have allowed us to better understand the world of human fertility, to learn about the possibilities which NFP presents for intimacy in the marriage relationship. We are sad to think that throughout our child-bearing years we never properly understood our own fertility, were never able to share that most intimate of moment of knowing fully that a conception was about to occur, did not truly realise that we are co-creators with God in the act of bringing into being a brand new person.

As with any sin, we can look back in regret and sorrow; but we have experienced very powerfully God's love and mercy, so we live in the present in true peace. We look ahead to many opportunities to share the message of *Humanae Vitae*, as we continue to grow into it ourselves, to live it and to be totally open to the new spiritual life that has awakened within us.

Fifteen

A Day in a Catholic Marriage

by Catherine Fournier

5:30 am. *Ehn-Ehn-Ehn.* The alarm jolts me awake. I cross the bedroom and tap the snooze button on the clock. I stumble back to bed, grope for the thermometer and stick it in my mouth. My movements awaken Peter slightly. He reaches across the bed and shakes my shoulder gently, 'Time . . . take your temperature Cat', he mumbles. I don't answer, my mouth is already full of the thermometer.

It has taken us a long time to become comfortable with NFP, to share the responsibility of it. For years, we struggled with an undercurrent of tension over who would 'run' our fertility; I driven by a need to control every aspect of my life and a fear of pregnancy, Peter by a fear of rejection and a wish for greater intimacy. Now he participates by reminding me each morning, asking me about other symptoms in the evening and studying the chart intensely every month beginning about Day 16. Every month we learn to trust, love and live together a little better.

5:48 am. The alarm goes off for the third time. Peter gets up to turn it all the way off. He comes back to bed, 'How are you feeling this morning, love? Do you want to stay in bed a bit longer?'

I stretch cautiously feeling my joints protest, 'Just a few more minutes'.

6:30 am. I wake up when Peter comes back into the bedroom. He climbs back into bed for a quick hug. These morning hugs are important, they help us stay aware of each other through our long busy day. Then we both get up. While Peter dresses for work, I make coffee and his lunch. I hang the lunch bag on the front door knob. This is the only way to make sure his lunch goes with him when he leaves for work. I leave everything else on the counter and set breakfast food on the kitchen table.

6:45 am. If I'm quick and lucky, I can beat the teenager rush and have a shower. I glance at the card of Our Lady of Combermere stuck into the switch plate as I turn on the light in the bathroom. It reminds me who this day belongs to.

Lord, take all of my thoughts and works and intentions of this day and use them for your purposes. I offer the pain of today for your priests.

7:00 am. On my way out of the bathroom, I look in on sixteen year old Tina, four year old Robert and seven year old Jonathon to be sure they are awake. On my way downstairs to where our bedroom is, I check that Sarah, eleven, Matthew, nine, and Andrew are awake too. This morning I need to shake Andrew and speak very loudly. He is fourteen, growing fast and always tired.

Guardian angels, wake up! Guard my children today, keep them from harm.

Grant me patience, Lord. Help me to keep smiling, even when I'm frustrated.

7:10 am. Peter calls 'Good-bye everyone!' The smaller children come running for a hug. He pats his pockets to be sure he has his rosary, his wallet, his ID badge, his cigarettes, gives me one last kiss and goes out to sweep the snow off his car.

8:00 am. The children leave to catch the bus. 'Bye, Mom, have a good day!' they call. 'Bye, guys!' I answer. 'Be kind to your teachers!'

While I clean up the kitchen and eat my breakfast, I plan what we'll have for dinner. Today is Monday, so it's beans night. Last Wednesday was chicken night and I have chicken stock, so I could make hot and sour soup with lots of tofu. Last week I made baked beans, and there's a meal's worth in the freezer ready but I'll save it for a busier Monday.

8:30 am. Time to start the morning tidy. Organisation is my defence against incurable scatterbrained-ness. I always follow some kind of routine to be sure that I don't forget a job.

You know my biggest failing, Lord, that I'd rather spend the day reading a book than working. I forget everything else: the time, the laundry, dinner, everything. It's selfish and a misuse of my time. Help me remember who my time and my work are for before I pick up a book.

I do a tidying sweep through the house twice a day. The house is organised enough that everything has its own place, and it runs fairly smoothly when I make sure that everything is in its place. I pick up the children's books, clothes and dropped papers and deliver them to their rooms. It sometimes makes me angry; I work so hard to make a pleasant home for them and all they do is mess it up. I resent tidying. Then I notice that everyone makes a mess whether I am angry about it or not, and I remember that all being angry does is make our home an unpleasant place.

Tidying has another purpose. Besides making our home a comfortable, pleasant place to live and work in, it gives the children an example of how to work. If I am conscientious about my work, doing it as cheerfully and completely as I can even if I don't always manage that too well, remember, I'd rather be reading, the children will learn what I have learned, that all work can be performed as an offering to God, that we can take pride and satisfaction in any job done well. Housework may seem an endless succession of insignificant little jobs but I've found that if I neglect just one task for too long the whole atmosphere of the home changes.

This work is one of the ways I have to serve you, Lord. You made housework, just like you made every other kind of work, so it must be important. Even if I don't always see its value. Help me to remember to do all my work with love, care and attention. Especially when I don't see its value.

Next, I start the laundry. I don't have much to do today, just one load of wet bed sheets. I used to do three or four loads of laundry a day. I got clothes mixed up between kids and of course socks always went missing. So I decided about a year ago that they were old enough to do it themselves and needed the responsibility. I assigned a day for each bedroom and now I only take care of the youngest boys, and Peter and myself.

There's such a balance to reach, isn't there Mary? Between doing things for your children, and doing too much. Between letting them be responsible for themselves and still being responsible for them. I chose you for my Mother, help me to be the mother my children need me to be.

When I go downstairs, Robert follows me. He likes to help me hang up the laundry in front of the wood stove. His conversation is a constant stream of questions: Is it tomorrow? How do busses work? What are raisins? When is Dad coming home? Could I have a cookie now?

After fifteen minutes, my brain aches.

9:45 am. Now that we've finished hanging up the laundry, it's time to tidy the bedrooms. I go down the hall, look into Matthew and Andrew's room, tiptoe in to turn off the light and the radio and leave again. I shudder and close the door. Sarah's room same thing. What I don't see, I don't itch to clean. We've agreed that they have to take care of their rooms themselves. This will also teach them responsibility and self-discipline. Eventually. I hope.

Lord, grant me patience. Now!

10:00 am. I don't have any errands to do this morning. Instead, I bring out some puzzles and colouring books, and turn on a children's programme for Robert before I go into my office. Turning on the computer, I sit down to write. I love writing; besides raising children, it is the most difficult and the most satisfying thing I've ever done.

Writing involves sacrifices for the whole family. I always feel a little guilty about Robert watching TV instead of doing something more educational. I don't have time to clean anymore, we all houseclean on the weekends instead of me taking care of it through the week. The time I spend writing I don't spend baking, sewing or fixing things around the house, all the things that help us to save money and live on one salary. We've had to scrimp a little harder since I started writing.

Holy Spirit, guide my fingers. Let what I write be your message in my stories.

11:59 am. Robert comes into the office. He is growing so tall, his eyes reach my shoulder when he stands beside my chair. 'Mom', he says. 'D'ya know what?' 'Oh, hi, honey', I answer, suddenly realising the time and that I'm hungry. Robert must be hungry too. I reach out and curl my arm around him. 'What?'

'I love you', he says softly, his eyes twinkling.

'I love you too', I answer, hugging him harder. 'You're my favourite Robert'. I kiss his cheek, feeling the delicate bones beneath his soft, soft, skin.

'And you're my favouritest Mom', he says.

Oh God, what did I do to deserve this? Surely it's not just by being a mother that I've earned this painful joy? My children are so much of me, and so much themselves at the same time. They fill my day, pound on my ears and tug at my arms with needs, demands, questions, wishes and dreams, with fun and laughter and joyful purpose too. Lord, help me always be the mother they need.

I go into the living room to turn the TV off. The news is on. Sue Rodriguez died by a doctor assisted suicide this weekend. It hurts me. 'Oh, you poor silly lady', I say and switch off the TV.

God, forgive them, I hope they know not what they do.

Rooting around in the drawer under our prayer table, I find the votive candles and light one for Sue Rodriguez. Our prayer table, or family altar, is a small wooden cupboard that stands in the corner between our living room and dining room. During Advent, our Jesse tree stands there, where it can be seen from anywhere on the ground floor. Other times of the year, a statue of Mary, a plaque of the Holy Family, our rosary book, the Bible, a votive candle holder and vases of flowers crowd our prayer table. I hang our banners on the wall above it; our saint's day banner, our Advent banner, our Easter banner.

12:30 pm. The phone rings. Peter has called to say hello. This is something we've done for as long as he's been working; either I call him or he calls me. Our morning hug keeps us aware of each other; our phone calls keep us in touch as a couple and as a parent team working together to raise our kids.

Lord, help me to be the wife my husband needs, to never take his presence, help and support for granted.

1:00 pm. Once we've finished lunch, the afternoon passes quickly. Robert and I wash dishes, make some cookies for an after-school snack, then he plays with his blocks while I work at the knitting machine on a sweater I'm making for Peter.

4:00 pm. Before I know it, the afternoon is over; the dog is barking frantically as the school bus pulls away. Snow-covered children pour into the house, hungry and full of news. Sarah has the mail. Tina tracks muddy snow across the kitchen floor again. Jonathon proudly announces that he has homework.

Help me, Mary; this is the most difficult part of my day. You know I hurt, you know the children are tired and hungry; you know how quickly tempers can flare, how quickly I can lose patience. Help us all feel your peaceful presence, and help me be the mother my children need.

While the children have a snack and do their homework, I cut up vegetables, mix the seasonings for the hot and sour soup and put a pot of rice on to cook. Suddenly, there is shouting and thumping downstairs. From the sound of Sarah and Andrew's voices, I know this argument will get out of control, so I hurry down. A shoving match has developed over a computer catalogue. Sarah is always sure she's right, and Andrew hasn't learned to control his temper very well yet.

I find fights and rudeness very hard to cope with; sometimes keeping my own temper is difficult. This time, I suddenly know exactly what to do. Separating the children, I deliberately rip up the catalogue. I calmly tell them they can order another one when they can stop fighting about it.

I know I haven't solved their disagreement for them, and fighting is an unavoidable part of growing up. All I can do is steer them towards the discovery that fighting is remarkably inefficient, and not Christ-like. To be happy, productive, faithful adults, somehow they must learn that people are always more important than things.

But I always wonder, is knowing this myself enough? Do I teach this by words or by example? Is allowing them to fight at all a good example?

In this and so many other things, they are in your hands, Lord.

5:00 pm. I return upstairs, just in time to save the rice from burning. Dinner is ready and Peter will be home soon. I'm very tired so I lie down on the couch. Robert bounces into the living room and lies down on my stomach. Jon curls up against my feet. Matthew is lying on the floor drawing a fox. Tina is still at the dining room table finishing her homework. Jon reads us all a story. When he's finished, he gets up and lays his head on my chest.

'I love you, Mom', he whispers. Seven year old big boys need to be shy about expressing such things. 'You're a good Mom'.

'Thank you, honey', I answer, patting his head. 'You're a good Jonathon'.

Again, I feel that delicious stab of painful joy. Thank you, Lord, for the tremendous gift of my children.

5:59 pm. 'Dad's home!' Sarah shouts, coming up the stairs. 'Daddy, Daddy!' A thunder of feet to the front door. I get up from the couch and join the hug line. Peter and I won't have time for anything else until the little ones are in bed.

'Jonathon, would you please set the table, maybe Robert can help you. Matthew, would you go and tell Andrew that dinner is ready, please? How was your day, Peter?'

Matthew plays a game every evening at dinner. While everyone is talking, telling us about their day, Matthew doesn't say anything. His private game is to see if anyone will notice. He's a very quiet hidden child. So I ask him, 'Matthew, did you learn anything interesting at school today? Is there anything you want to talk about?'

He looks at me. 'No', he says and begins to giggle. I noticed, and he thinks it's funny. What a special child; he doesn't exactly keep his light under a bushel, but he definitely shields it.

Tina and Andrew want to talk about euthanasia and suicide; the Sue Rodriguez story has been discussed at school. Most of the children at school apparently think that people should have the right to suicide. Peter and I glance at each other, take a deep breath and start.

'Well first of all, let's look at the word 'right.' What is a 'right?' What would make people think suicide was a right?' We appreciate these opportunities to talk with our kids. We feel thankful that our children bring these concerns to us. One by one, the younger children ask permission to leave the table. I remind them to wash their faces, brush their teeth and 'pajamanise' themselves. This always makes them giggle.

8:00 pm. Dishes are washed, stories are read, homework finished and put away. Time for prayers. It's so much of a tradition now that the children won't go to bed without prayers. We pray a decade of the rosary, a Hail Holy Queen and finish with a prayer that Peter invented: 'My Guardian Angel, thanks for keeping me safe and helping me be a good (*Name*) all day long. Help me pay attention to Mommy and Daddy and whoever's looking after me all day tomorrow. Amen'.

9:00 pm. After an hour of talking about our day, it's time for me to go to bed. I read for a little while, and then I turn out the light and think. There is so much that I didn't do, so much that I could've done, should've done. I need to pray more, alone and with Peter, not just evening prayers with the children. I should read better books, lives of saints, Scripture, meditations. I make these resolutions every night, yet I only seem to be creeping towards accomplishing what I know I must do for the good of my family and myself. Well, what *did* I do today?

What some people would think of as another ordinary uneventful day, even boring or demeaning, has gone by, full of enormous events, sparkling with teaching moments. I know I've done more than tidy, scrub pots, wipe spills and listen to stories and questions. I've spent the day building our family.

Goodnight Jesus.

Sixteen

Snow and Roses

by Joan Barrow

'That's it. I've had it. I can't take anymore. The next catastrophe, problem complaint, criticism, excuse or idiotic phone call and I'm out of here! I'm tired of one irritation after another. I'm fed up with self-centred people and the schemers and manipulators of the world. That's it!'

Sound familiar? Most of us have uttered that little tirade, either vocally or mentally, a number of times. We have all experienced this type of stress in our lives in one form or another.

One year, our family experienced an inordinate number of rather stressful situations. Like most family satires, it takes on almost a cartoon effect in the retelling so many years after it happened.

In those years, the early 1960s, we lived on a small farm in eastern Ontario. It had been cut from the bush by my husband's Irish parents who had settled there in the 1800s. The old oak log beams of our little house were so heavy they had gradually sunk the building deep about a 10 degree angle. There was no running water and we had an 'out-house' that was full of 'character'!

We didn't have much security in those years. My husband worked part-time on the railroad to supplement the farm's small income. We didn't need much; there was always lots of good food to eat, although little actual money. I treasured the baskets of crab apples we gathered on the edge of the woods in the autumn. The sound of the winter wind singing around the corners of the house was good company. I delighted in the beautiful, snow covered fields, appreciated the sound of frogs and crickets on a spring night as an evening at the symphony. The wild rose-bushes growing along the back fence in summer were my special joy.

And people, people of all kinds came to visit, family and strangers by the car loads. We always loved visiting. One summer we had four hundred guests; we counted. Our old upright piano provided lots of entertainment. We prayed the rosary every night and went off to Mass in our broken-down Ford every Sunday come hell or high water. And there were children and so much love in our family it never really crossed our minds that we were somewhat hard up.

One special Christmas we didn't have much cash for 'bought presents'. My four year old daughter Jane and two year old son Dennis helped me make cookies. They wrapped them up carefully for gifts to each other. I secretly knit socks for Steve's present. Seven pairs, one for each day of the week, each of them a different colour and design. I made mitts and scarves for the children and on Christmas morning you should have seen the delight on their faces. Then Steve presented me with a little china lady in a plastic case. She came with a note: 'To my wife, a lady who makes everyday life seem exotic and out of the ordinary'.

I didn't realise it then, but a period of our life that was quite out of the ordinary was about to begin. On New Year's Day, Steve, the children and I, expecting our third child Helen, left after dinner with our relatives to return home. It was a very cold winter's night and the heater in the car did not work. I reached into the back seat, lifted the two children into the front and wrapped a blanket around them. We were all laughing, in a holiday mood.

We stopped at a red traffic light. Within seconds, the car lurched forward with a tremendous, explosive, crashing noise. We had been hit from behind by a car that had failed to stop. As the impact drove into a large, steel girder, I grabbed the blanket, pulled the children in close and leaned over them in protection. The crash demolished the back seat of the car, and the front looked like an accordion. The impact knocked Steve unconscious, snapped the seat under me and broke my lower back. The children had some bruises, but otherwise were not seriously injured.

The accident marked the beginning of some very difficult times. Thankfully, Helen was born in good health. Although there was no permanent injury to my spine, I could not walk for a few months and wore a back brace for two years. Our family offered a prayer of thanks that none of us had been killed.

Shortly after the accident, a railway strike was called, leaving employees off work for over two months without pay. After the strike had finally been settled, on a rainy night, a colleague failed to see Steve standing at the top of a box car and gave the all-clear hand signal. The engineer shunted the box cars forward, throwing my husband to the ground. Despite an injury to his back and leg, Steve continued working, unable to bear the thought of being unemployed again.

Our small berry business, which provided some additional income, suffered. Neither of us could physically pick berries, and we could not find pickers to hire, as we lived in an isolated area. Our financial difficulties were getting more severe each day. In addition to this list of calamities, a friend accidentally tripped over the new water pipe and broke it; we had just installed it after years of carrying water by bucket from the hand-pump across the yard. The whole downstairs of the farm house flooded. The humour of the situation struck us; we actually sat down and laughed. Until we could afford to fix the water line, however, we were back to carrying water from the well during those cold winter months. But the hard luck didn't stop. An exceptionally heavy snowfall that year aggravated our situation. The car broke down every time we looked at it. Disaster seemed to follow disaster.

One day, I sat at the kitchen table, waiting for some pies to bake in the oven. I prayed as the baby perched on my knee. If anyone had peeked in the door it would have looked like a homely, pastoral scene, but I had finally reached the end of my endurance. I stormed heaven for help.

Suddenly, as I prayed, a knock came at the door. I opened it to see a tall, handsome stranger. He smiled and asked to speak to my husband. Steve was not at home. The stranger gave me his card and asked if my husband would call as soon as possible. He was an engineer representing a radio station from Montreal, but he looked exactly like a guardian angel to me.

The happy ending of this story is that the radio company bought the back field of the farm for a transmitter station. Our financial difficulties were over. Our prayers had been answered in a very dramatic, dynamic way.

My husband and I both got down on our knees that night and fervently thanked God for his help. God's providence underlined for us what Jesus told us in the Sermon on the Mount: 'Ask and you will receive. Seek and you will find. Knock and it will be opened to you'.

We could not control the factors that contributed to stress in our lives during that time. However, as each problem disappeared one by one, the memory of the pain and anxiety also disappeared. Our hard times didn't miraculously cease after that incident. Other difficulties followed: as I walked along a street at night some time later, a reckless driver veered towards me at top speed. I stepped backward to escape and fell into a deep culvert. As a result I lost the baby twins we were expecting. Then, I developed heart problems while still in childrearing years. Steve died of cancer when our youngest children, Helen and Joe, were still in school. I had to work to support the family. I sold the farm eventually and moved to the city. I've been operated on for cancer and had open-heart surgery twice. But from these trials I've learned that we can *choose* to be pessimists, optimists or realists. We can learn to treat each individual worry as just that, an individual situation. When stress threatens to overwhelm us, we should take constructive action. The simple set of guidelines below have helped me to not only handle the stress of daily life, but also appreciate my life and the lives of those around me:

Endure as best we can life's small annoyances.

Handle problems before they become major issues.

Enjoy life's many blessings to the fullest.
Bring humour and laughter back into our lives.
Love our neighbour as ourselves.
Ask for God's help and never forget the power of prayer.

Seventeen

I Will if I Have To, But Please Don't Ask Me

by Catherine Fournier

One very ordinary early spring morning in 1994. The sun shone, the ice had begun to melt off the roof, the birds were singing again, but I was not having a good day. For one thing, Robert was in the living room watching *The Return of the Jedi* for the 57th time. I thought I'd scream.

I'd been in my office all morning, in a housecoat and no slippers, searching for a manuscript: the only copy of a story submitted to the *Nazareth Journal*, lost. I worried away the night about it and went through my morning routine with more than half my mind on the chaos of paper in the office. At 11:30, I finally admitted defeat and climbed into the shower. The phone rang. I thought about screaming again.

It was Peter, my husband. His calling in the middle of the day was unusual. At one time we spoke everyday at lunch, but increasing responsibilities, his recent promotion to a managerial position and two business trips in the last month had swallowed his moments of free time and much of our weekends too. I missed the moment to moment contact that is so important between spouses and so necessary to the running of a large family, but we had carefully considered this promotion and were confident that the workload would reduce to manageable proportions within a year. Peter felt guilty enough being away from his family so much, so I chose not to increase his guilt by saying that I found it difficult without him. I let him take care of himself and his workload, while I ran the house and took care of the family.

Even though dripping wet with shampoo running down my face, I was glad he called.

The back ground noises are unusual, I thought in the instant before he spoke. *Is he calling from a meeting that I didn't know about?*

'Hi, Cat', he said. 'Do you know where I am?' His voice was curiously flat and . . . hurt.

Should I know where he is? I wonder. *Oh gosh, was I supposed to meet him?*

'I'm at the hospital', he said, voice still flat and expressionless, 'they think I've had a heart attack'.

A great ringing silence suddenly descended over some vital portion of my brain. The sun shone, water ran down my back, Han Solo yelled something to Chewbacca and my husband has just told me that he may have been near death.

Don't sound upset, I thought, *he needs me not to be upset.*

'Where are you?' I asked, in the same curiously flat unemotional tone he used.

'The Queensway Carleton. Look, I have to go now', he answered with the slightest upward quaver. The phone rattled, I heard the rustle of clothing, then a nurse's voice.

'Are you finished now, Mr. Fournier? Can I help you back?' and the phone line cut off. I stood, frightened.

My husband, no, my life, my world, always so strong, capable and dependable, is suddenly so sick he needed a nurse's help to get up from a chair. *Be calm, cope, be calm, cope. No, I can't, I need help. Who can I turn to?*

I called our friend Sandra at her workplace, and shook and cried. She said she'd meet me in the nearby town of Arnprior and drive me to the hospital in Ottawa.

I called another friend, Teri, shook and cried again. She offered to take the kids for as long as necessary.

I called the school, managed not to cry, arranged for the kids to go from school to Teri's house.

Have I thought of everything? . . . No.

I called Madonna House, talked to Father Bob, shook and cried, blurted out what I had been trying not to think, 'He can't die! He can't leave me now!'

Yes, he can.

I asked for prayers, asked that word be spread for prayers.

What next?

Still dazed and numb, my mind moved slowly. I packed the children's pyjamas and clothes, dressed Robert, dressed myself. I got into the car to drop Robert and bags of clothes at Teri's house, then to meet Sandra.

I drove for a long time before my brain caught up with my body. Only then, did I think of praying. I began automatically:

'Our Father, who art in Heaven, hallowed by thy Name. Thy will be done . . . .'

Thy will be done, Lord? Even this?

My life is in your hands, Lord, and so is Peter's. I know that. No buts. I can't beg you to spare his life. If you want him now, I can't argue.

Can you really ask me to live the rest of my life without Peter? Do you really think I can? I don't. God, I will if I must, but please don't ask me to.

Is this how Christ felt?

But his suffering was worse, much worse.

There are moments in everyone's life that are remembered forever with great clarity. I remember grasping the concept of reading, I remember the moment I knew I loved Peter, I remember the first step of my conversion when I recognised my own sinfulness and I remember my 'Gethsemane moment'. It seemed to be endless. In a sense it was. I was terribly afraid, afraid for myself, afraid for the children, afraid Peter would die before I could travel the 60 kilometres to Ottawa, that we wouldn't have a chance to say 'Goodbye, see you later'. I wasn't afraid for Peter; there was nothing to be afraid of, for him.

I was in incredible pain, the indescribable pain of heartbreak and loss. I could hardly breathe. This man had been part of my life since I was fifteen years old, my friend, my mentor, my helpmate, my love. How could I go on with my heart and my right arm missing? I also felt ashamed. I had been so busy with the house, with the children, with feeling lonely and sorry for myself, that I hadn't known anything was wrong with Peter. How could I love him and not see this coming? How could I have neglected him and taken him for granted so? I just always thought he'd be there. Had Peter gotten sick because I had relied on him past his endurance? Had I made Peter the centre of my life instead of God? Was this why God was taking him away from me? Yet I was calm, calm that whatever happened was meant to happen, that whatever happened all I had to do was 'the next thing'.

Even if the next thing is . . . ?

In the years since my conversion, God has taught me over and over again that my life is not in my control. Car accidents, children's illnesses, children's accidents, financial chaos, extended peacefulness when I, slowly and reluctantly, handed over portions of my life into God's hands.

'You want the kids? Well, they are your children after all. Okay, God, I place my children in your hands'.

'You can see the whole picture, Lord, I can't. I will trust you that our money will turn out all right'.

But I always, even when I didn't realise that I was doing so, kept part of myself back. Why? Out of fear, I guess, at what might happen if I let God 'make the decisions'. Who knew what he might ask me to accept?

This for one thing.

I learned that day that my control of my life was an illusion. What I thought of as 'control' was a white-knuckled grip on something too large for me to grasp. Only God's hands are strong enough to steer a safe course. Nothing and no one would always be there, except God. Nothing and no one could take care of me and love me forever, except God. Only at that moment, when

I recognised the illusion of control I had been making, could I finally and truly place all of my life, all of myself, all my hopes, prayers, plans, everything, into God's hands, trusting his guidance and grace.

Before this 'Gethsemane moment', that moment of *I will, Lord, if you ask it of me. But if you can, please don't ask me.*

Trust in God seemed a perilous and risky thing. But at that moment of choice and surrender, and since, I have found that trust in God is the only certain thing in an uncertain life.

I am sure that everyone has such a moment in their life. Maybe there are many moments in every life, or maybe every moment is the moment. It does seem to me, though, that a moment of clear and unavoidable choice is inevitable. Life is so full of choices; mishap, adventure, love or intellect will eventually lead us to the only real choice, to accept or reject the reality of God's will in our life.

As you may have guessed, Peter did not die. He hadn't had a heart attack, but in the words of the doctors in the emergency ward, 'a darn good imitation' brought on by overwork and stress. He spent five days in the hospital, two weeks at home, and two months working half time before he returned to a full time schedule. It took about a year for a complete recovery, a year of adjustment for both of us. We both had to learn to admit that we couldn't 'do it all', to give up the illusion of control and give our lives over to God. And to rely on each other, as God-given spouses, more.

Peter promised to tell me when he was feeling stressed, and I promised to take better care of him. A promise that I promptly broke. That autumn, Robert, our youngest child, was badly scalded with hot tea, suffering second and third degree burns to ten percent of his body. Two days later, our oldest boy Andrew, hugged his father too hard and cracked two of his ribs. Totally focused on my bandaged boy, I left the poor, wounded, shallowly-breathing man to fend for himself. He even had to drive himself to the emergency department. It's always something new, and it's always the same thing.

Eighteen

Quietly Running Taps

by Catherine Fournier

That it took me by surprise, I can only explain this way: I'm the oldest of three girls; children of only children. My sisters and I grew up with no cousins or uncles. My father travelled in the Arctic from May to October. Our household was usually my mother, my sisters, my great aunt, a female cat and myself. Most of the children I baby-sat were girls. I had no experience of boys at all before our hyperactive first son Andrew was born. I had no inkling of how a little boy's mind works and I still never quite know what they'll do next.

The stories that my husband Peter's family tells about itself had given me some idea of what to expect. My father-in-law was shot through the leg with a .22 while playing cops and robbers when he was thirteen. His brothers sent a truck tire through a department store window when a game on a steep hill got out of hand. Peter set the garage on fire while filling a gas lawnmower when he was about twelve. At the same age, he climbed a tree carrying his large, and agitated, German Shepherd. My militia brother-in-law put his foot through the floor practising marching when he was seventeen. My husband's other brother, in a hurry to catch the school bus, left a cat, a dog and a squirrel in a live trap in the living room all day, though the squirrel didn't stay in the live trap and the animals didn't stay in the living room. As I told a father of two young boys a few weeks ago, 'Don't get too fond of your furniture'.

I guess that's why it was such a shock when eight year old Andrew flooded the house. I'd expected something involving bandages, but not this.

We left the house on a summer Saturday morning to spend the weekend visiting grandparents. Peter and I always do a last minute check through the house, for safety's sake, making sure that windows are closed and locked and that appliances are safely turned off. We returned, in time for the last Sunday Mass at our home parish. Andrew met a school friend at church and asked to go home with Billy to play for the afternoon.

Peter is always the first to go into the house while I start to unload the car. When he came back to the car, too soon I thought, he asked if I was tired.

'No'. I said, 'Not especially, why?'

'Well, Cat, you've had a rough week and I thought maybe you'd like to go and visit your mother'.

'Peter, I know you too well. What's wrong? Was the house broken into? Is it a mess? What?!!'

'No, the house wasn't broken into exactly; it's just sort of . . . wet in there and I thought maybe you'd like to go see your mother.' The poor man made a desperate attempt to save us all from what was coming. Total Mom Meltdown. 'You don't want to see it, really.'

Of course, I had to see for myself. I ran across the driveway and up to the house. As soon as I got to the front door, I heard the most sickening sound. Water poured from the ceiling onto sodden carpet already dark with water and littered with the remains of the living room ceiling. I screamed, and a piece of plaster peeled off the wall and splashed on the floor.

Peter joined me at the front door, continuing his effort to steer me from hysterics. 'I told you that you didn't want to see it. You can still go visit your mother.' I ignored him.

Obviously, the water was coming from the bathroom, so I ran up the stairs. I screamed again. It was worse upstairs. The bathroom, at least an inch deep in water, floated in vinyl tiles. A stream ran from the bathroom across the hall and disappeared into gaps between the warped hardwood flooring of our bedroom. My beautiful bedroom floor looked like corrugated roofing. I waded into the bathroom. A tap quietly ran into an overflowing sink.

The sink was overflowing because the plug was in the drain and a face cloth stuffed into the overflow drain. I thought some child must have, uncharacteristically, been washing his face before we left for our visit, and the cloth had *somehow* floated into the overflow drain.

The mess was indescribable, almost unfathomable in its totality. There were puddles in the *basement*. The bookcase in the living room burst from the pressure of sodden swollen curtain tracks out of the walls. The plaster walls flowed and slumped like melting ice cream.

Peter and I moved the furniture into the only dry room left on the ground floor, the kitchen. We borrowed a wet vacuum machine and sucked up twenty gallons of water before we acknowledged defeat, ripped up the carpet and pushed it out of the window. The children carried their sopping toys out of the basement and arranged them on the back lawn to dry. All the while, my mind whirled in helpless circles, like a panicked mouse, trying to figure out *how* this had happened and what to do next.

All I could think was, 'The Old Testament had a flood story and now so do we'.

Still shaking from the shock and the exertion of pulling up the wet living room carpet, I went to pick up Andrew at Billy's house. There I learned the truth. I apologised to Andrew for hurrying him and explained it was because we had a bit of a problem at home; a tap had accidentally been left running and the house was a total mess.

'Oh no', Andrew said softly to himself.

'Oh no? What do you mean – Oh no?' I demanded. Andrew sank lower into the car seat.

'Oh Andrew, don't tell me you did this', I pleaded.

'Well, yes Mom. I did do it', he confessed. 'I'm really sorry.'

'But Andrew . . . why? I don't understand! Why would you do something like that?' I wailed, struggling between keeping my mind on driving the car and wanting to throttle him.

'I just wanted to see what would happen.'

It wasn't a very good reason, was it? Still, it was all the reason he could ever give. Horrified when he saw the state of the house, Andrew offered to sell all his possessions to pay the damages. He helped late into the night moving furniture and carrying out wet plaster. He and the rest of the family lived with the inconvenience of the long cleanup, the unpredictable coming and going of carpenters, plasterers and carpet layers. As much as he tried, he could never explain his motivation any better than that first desperate confession. He wondered what would happen and, being unable to visualise it, opted for the experimental method.

It took me years to be able to see this story for anything more than an addition to the Fournier legends, but recently I began to understand it differently. One of our family Advent readings was the story of Noah's Ark. I suddenly saw a similarity between Andrew's ineffectual explanation and the genesis of sin, the persistence of sin that so outraged God that he sent a flood to wash all mortal life away.

Andrew is a clever boy. He imagined a situation and wondered what would happen. Because of his age and his temperament, he couldn't visualise the consequences, so he decided to experiment. He followed his own will and his own judgement. The results were disastrous.

Our free will and intellect, given to us by God, make us able to imagine all kinds of situations. We wonder what will happen if we act upon those impulses. But as heirs of original sin, we have inherited imperfect bodies, intellects and wills; it is not within our power to be aware of all the physical, mental and spiritual ramifications of our actions. It is easy to decide that these consequences do not exist at all. This is called pride. In pride we decide to follow our own will and judgement. The results are just as disastrous as Andrew's experiment.

No matter how hard we try, our efforts will always fail to create a perfectly balanced, permanently peaceful society. In pride, we follow our own will and judgement. We keep trying to learn solely from our own mistakes, even though history makes it quite clear that we have never done a good job of learning from mistakes, especially the mistakes of others.

When Andrew imagined the situation of the plug, the face cloth and the quietly running tap and wondered what would happen, he thought he had two choices. Since he couldn't visualise the results, he could either leave the puzzle, or solve it through experimentation. Andrew forgot that he had a third option. He could have asked us. We knew what would happen, we could have explained it to him, and given him many reasons not to do it.

It's very funny, now, to tell of the little boy who briefly considered and impulsively acted. An innocent child, barely at an age to be responsible for his actions, made a big mistake. There is no culpability in the story, there hardly seems to be any point in telling it except for its humour. Yet isn't this what sin *is*, wondering what will happen and opting for the experimental method?

We are not innocent children and we are responsible for our actions and all the consequences, seen and unseen. Our culpability lies in the fact that in pride we forget that we, too, have a third option. We sin as easily as we think, especially when we make the mistake of thinking that we can decide the ethical and moral value of an action based solely on what we can visualise and perceive for ourselves.

Andrew's experimentation has shown me that it's not so much the great sins that we have to guard against in ourselves. It's the small acts of pride, easily overlooked, the tiny impulsive actions taken without remembering our third option that are so very dangerous, because they lead to bigger things. Each little sin numbs us to, and finally chokes off, our awareness of sins. The daily, barely noticed venial sins; the little burst of impatience, the nurtured doubt, the destructive habits, are all quietly running taps.

Nineteen

The House That Love Built

by Geraldine Hertz

In the middle of the night, as we all slept in the upstairs of the old, draughty farmhouse, a strange feeling woke me. Maybe it's a spider, I thought. You can't be sure in this old, rickety house. I switched on the bed lamp and drew back in horror. There, standing with forepaws against the sheet, stood a huge grey rat, and the sheet was wet where it had been drooling against my ear.

'Joe!' I gasped. 'Do something!'

Joe took one groggy look and leaped out of bed. The rat ambled a few feet away, thoroughly unafraid. His utter unconcern, as though we were the intruders in his domain, staggered us. Joe grabbed a tube from the Electrolux standing against the wall. He gave a mighty swing at the rat, smashed my bedroom scales into bits, bent the vacuum cleaner tube and missed the rat.

The moth-eaten animal jumped into a half-open dresser drawer and glared at us, revealing sharp teeth in a snarl of contempt. I snuck out the bedroom door. With the door nearly closed, I peeked back in.

'Go downstairs and bring my .22', Joe said quietly. 'Then next time I won't miss.'

I hurried down the chilly hall and into the damp downstairs where my father slept. I could just imagine what he would think if he woke up in the night as a shot went off in our bedroom.

I shook my father's shoulder until he wakened, and explained that if he heard a shot, Joe was just killing a rat. Dad nodded and sat up in bed, lighting his pipe.

Going to the gun cabinet, I took the pistol, hurried upstairs and passed it through the door to Joe. Quietly and carefully, he aimed. Slowly, he pulled the trigger. The rat jumped from the drawer, the bullet hit him in mid-air and he dropped. I flung the door open, checking to be certain he was dead.

'Get the dustpan to carry him out, some paper towels and bleach water', Joe said. 'He didn't bleed much.'

I shuddered and went downstairs again.

'It's okay, Pop', I said. 'Now go to sleep and we'll see you in the morning.'

Good advice, but when the rodent had been disposed of, I couldn't take it. How do you lie your head down on a pillow stained with fresh rat drool?

I sat for awhile on the edge of the bed, and then hunted out fresh sheets, fresh bleach water for the mattress and even fresh blankets. And still I couldn't sleep. Not only was I revolted by rats, but my eighteen month old baby had been sleeping peacefully not ten feet from where the rat had been. What if he'd spit up a little, and the rat decided to nibble against his ear? I knew the horrible statistics, that many children lose ears or parts of fingers in this way every year right here in America. I was determined that we would leave this old ramshackle house.

I spent the rest of the night in the kitchen making plans. When Joe came downstairs in the morning, I set his coffee and waffle before him. My father joined us in our breakfast before the children awoke. This can be the quietest, nicest time of the day. Our ten children would soon be coming down, and then the early morning stillness would dissolve like a mist in the sunshine.

But this morning neither the rising crescendo of awakening children nor the warmth of the spring morning outside could alleviate my dreadful knowledge that we lived in a slum. Never mind that the creek gurgled not twenty feet from the kitchen window. And never mind the freedom of the farm for the children, and the advantages of running barefoot through spring grass and all the other blessings of growing up on the farm. Freedom from urban cares we had. But rats we had too.

'Joe', I began as I sat down opposite him, 'we've got to have a new house'.

The bite of waffle stopped halfway to his mouth. He didn't answer right away. He was only 46, but this morning his shoulders slumped in a way I had never seen before.

'You know I want one too', he said, 'but who'd ever loan us the money, when we have all these kids? You know I've tried.' His eyes were damp. His dark hair showed signs of grey at the temples, but he was still a handsome hardworking man.

'Joe, do you mind if I try? This isn't the first time those rats have scared me. But it's the first time they've been so bold. We need a house that's rat-proof.'

'Do what you like about it', he said, 'but in the meantime I'll get some rat poison. That'll get rid of them again, at least for a while.'

I nodded. Poison made me uneasy, because it was hard to find places where a child could never possibly reach.

'Joe', Pop said as he joined us, 'I don't know whether you can get a loan to build, but if you do, then count me in. I'll build your cabinets and do other carpentry work that you'll let me.' Pop was a small determined man, and when he spoke you could always depend on him. Already I felt better. He had built several of the houses we'd lived in as I was growing up. Now retired, and a bit slow, anything he did was still done well.

Joe nodded as he left for work. As a longshoreman and part-time farmer, he always wanted good fences, good cattle and good machinery. He had given all his strength for his family and his farm, but still it was never enough, not with rising prices and the spiralling needs of our growing family.

We loved and wanted every single child God had given us, yet we had to admit that it cost to care for them. I smiled grimly as I heard the kids fighting about whose turn it was to use the bathroom.

'Stop it!' I commanded. 'Let Tom in first. He's the smallest!' And to myself I thought – two bathrooms. Now that's what we'll have in our new house!

Breakfast and getting children off to school took nearly two hours, but at last Pop and I had a quiet, leisurely cup of coffee while the preschoolers played.

'Would you mind the babies for me today and let me shop for a loan?' I asked.

'Okay', he answered. 'And take your time. I'll be drawing up a house plan you might like.'

I hurried upstairs and dressed very carefully. I knew that every prospective creditor would look me over closely and I had no wish to appear slovenly or shiftless. I shuddered at the words. They were too easily and too often applied to mothers or fathers of large families. No one ever seemed to consider that our marriage was a sacrament, that our children were the lucky children of a stable home.

It hadn't been easy to maintain any kind of serenity about being a big family, not with scientific advances questioning our every thought, word and deed. No one really appreciated that the security of our farm had kept us from ever needing or considering public assistance.

I didn't want charity this morning. I wanted the same opportunity for a loan that was offered eagerly to men and women with one or two children. I didn't want pity, and I couldn't let myself be turned down. Not this time. What I needed was a little 'social justice' for myself and my family.

Even so, I knew better than to begin with the banker who held the mortgage on our land. When Joe had asked him for a loan to build a new house months before, he laughed, 'Are you out of your mind? Who'd loan that kind of money to a man crazy enough to have ten kids?'

So it was my turn to make the rounds. But when I told the loan officers in the banks the size of my family, a visible haughtiness crept into their tones. During the following days of money-shopping, I covered nearly every credit organisation in the county, to be turned down by every one.

Yet nothing could erase my fear whenever I laid my head on my pillow at night. What of my children? It is possible to keep an old house clean, and it is possible to keep our children warm with the right clothing even in a draughty old house! Our children were healthy. But for how long? And what about that place under the sink where the floor had rotted away, the damp odour of the house, rising from the ground? The rank sourness of rotting timbers and mildewed wood?

Finally the Federal Land Bank man came out to see the farm for himself. After I listed our needs over a cup of coffee, he had to admit there was nothing he could do.

'Your husband makes the biggest part of his income from his job, and that makes him ineligible for a farm loan', he said. 'And while tree farming would qualify you in Alabama, it hasn't passed for this state.' He thanked me kindly, and walked toward the door.

But he was my last chance! If my own government, my own country, didn't believe in us, then who else would? And where was God when I needed him?

'Mr. Smith!' I said, praying for the right words as my chin thrust outward. 'Just a minute! Stop right there! Now please take a look at that bathroom door that's leaning against the wall! It fell off its hinges this morning. And take a look into the bathroom. Joe put a metal panel down so that we don't fall through the floor, because there's no good wood to nail new wood against. Everything turns to powder when he tries to nail into it. It's the same on the front porch. One of the children fell through up to his armpits yesterday. He wasn't hurt but he could have been killed! And come take a look under this sink. But don't just look. Smell it! I was not brought up to be either quiet or happy in a house like this, with the rats playing hopscotch through the attic every night. Someone has to do something! You can't just tell me *no* and dispose of my family that easily!' My voice shook.

I was ready to burst into tears, but I turned toward the stove and choked them back as I picked up the percolator and poured us some more coffee. Mr. Smith sat back down, a stunned look on his face.

'You're right, you know', he said, his blue eyes looking around with new perspective. 'Have you tried everyone?'

'Everyone'.

'The Farmers' Home Administration?'

'No. Are they in the phone book?'

He nodded. 'But they're under the US Government. And for them the one stipulation is that you must not be able to get credit from anyone else. Your problem with credit might just make you eligible for a loan at less interest than anyone else would charge.'

'You're kidding!' I said. I thanked him for the help. After he left I hurried to the phone book to make an appointment.

The application for a loan was filled out in April. In October, a man from Spokane came to the farm to consider our needs, and our house loan was verified shortly after that, but too late to build that year.

We were ecstatic. God had given us a chance to leave the old house. We drilled a new well in December, and throughout the winter, whenever there were a few days above freezing, Joe and the boys mixed small batches of cement and poured them into home-made forms for the foundation of our new fifteen-room house.

I remember trying to tell the FHA man that the house need not be that big, but he insisted they would not lend to build another slum. It had to be big enough for the size of the family.

Angela, our eleventh child, was born that same winter. But even so, I was able to spend time with the family, watching them mix cement and shovel into the rocky hillside for the basement of our new home.

One particularly warm winter day, blond, curly-haired Ron stopped digging for a moment and leaned against his shovel. At eleven he was not much help with his shovel, but he was willing. That day his eyes shone like blue crystal as he looked at me, then back at the foundation forms. 'Y'know, Mom', he said, 'I can hardly believe it's really happening. It doesn't seem real!'

'What makes you say that? This is America! People can do anything they set their minds to, God willing!'

'Yeah, I know. That's what the history books say, but it doesn't always turn out like that.'

'If it doesn't, then it's because someone hasn't tried hard enough!' I snapped.

He had hit a sore spot. True, that was the America I believed in, yet even so, we had nearly failed. And why? Even now years later, when I hear people grumbling at the high cost of welfare and taxes to help the homeless, I'm still proud of our family, and how it felt as all of us worked together! We had a sure-fire philosophy at our house. Pray like crazy, and then go for it!

The following July we began to build. I did all the painting, while Joe tarred the roof, with the help of our boys and the generous advice and tar pot of a professional roofer, a friend of ours.

Joe built the furnace, and helped with the plumbing. Together the kids and I laid vinyl tiles until everything was finished.

But God nudged us ahead of time. The Sunday before Thanksgiving, Joe stood at the bathroom mirror shaving, when a pipe inside the toilet tank broke. Water shot out from under the lid all over the floor. The boys handed Joe tools as he plugged the leak, then tried to see how much pipe he would need to repair the damage. But, like the rest of the house, there was nothing to repair against. The pipes had corroded away. The toilet became only a fixture, and Joe built a temporary outhouse until moving day.

We stepped up our work speed. Since the night of the rat, we were desperate to leave the old house. The previous year I had poisoned rats unmercifully: behind dressers, in pans in the attic and behind the freezer in the utility room. Anything or anywhere the baby couldn't move or crawl behind. I had become resigned to the job knowing that warfarin, because it causes internal bleeding, would give the rats a terrible thirst. They would leave the house and die beside the creek outside, to be disposed of safely.

But though I watched my toddlers carefully, the baby was learning to walk and sometimes got away from me. One rainy afternoon as I stirred stew in the kitchen, and while the older children were outside doing their chores, I suddenly felt a nagging, shivery feeling. Something was awfully wrong. Where was Bobby? I had seen him only minutes before, but now it was very quiet.

I went looking for him. He was in the living room, squatting behind the couch, pulling on the tail of a lethargic dying rat.

'Bobby!' I swooped him up under one arm and carried him into the bathroom for a thorough scrubbing. When the baby had been cleaned and the poisoned rat disposed of, I sat down and shook. 'O God, what will happen next?' I could not help being terrified and revolted. I wept until I had no more tears.

'Please God', I sobbed, 'help us finish this house! Our babies, too, have a right to be safe!'

We worked even harder, but never again did I let my baby out of my sight. Pop was nearly finished with the beautiful cabinets. I spent every day laying vinyl tiles to hurry the day we'd move. The older children helped after school. We finished a room a day, all but the corners, which needed both precision and strong hands. Joe finished the corners after work, and every evening a room's furniture was moved in, the children with it.

We finished moving on Thanksgiving Day, and celebrated our first meal in the big dining room. The smell of sage stuffing filled the house as Joe carried the golden brown turkey to the table and began to carve. The rest of us sat down around the table, ready to say grace. It is our custom every Thanksgiving to let each person tell what he or she is most thankful for.

This year it was unanimous. Our new house!

Eleven year old Ron looked at me across the table. 'Y'know, Mom, I never thought we'd make it. I can hardly believe it. I never thought we'd get the breaks, like other people do.'

In one succinct sentence he had exposed a greater threat than any rat: the effect of slum living on the minds of children. Joe and I never suspected that such damage was being done. Now as Joe, Pop and I exchanged glances, we knew that our old house, and our poverty, had given our kids a mistaken outlook on life. We had not prevented the easy acceptance of failure from seeping into their young minds. We'd both been competent and responsible parents. We had learned how much courage it takes to succeed in life. Yet, without realising, we had very nearly sent our children into the world without that most priceless gift God gives to his people: faith in him.

Our children knew the sting of poverty, the feel of the slum, but this new house, built by love, represented the grace of God; it showed our kids a vital proof that anything is possible, if we pray like crazy, then work at it. We'd built more than a house, we'd built a ladder to the stars for our children. Thank God for the rat which terrified me and started it all!

Twenty

Jesus Was an Only Child

by Astrid Nordholt

The Holy Family, Jesus, Mary and Joseph, is the ideal to which all Catholic families aspire. They are the model of holiness: in Mary we find the ideal wife and mother; Joseph models the vocations of father, protector and husband; Jesus is the one to whom we look as the perfectly obedient child.

The Holy Family, model of family life. And yet, in a sense, hardly typical. Mary's perpetual virginity is an article of the Catholic Faith. Joseph was the 'spouse most chaste'. Jesus had no brothers and sisters.

I, too, was an only child. I didn't recognise this fact until age six; none of my playmates had siblings. Wartime London saw many dads leaving moms behind with their first child. The war ended when I was five. Soon after, my friend Pat boasted a baby sister. The event is etched in my memory because Diana was the first tiny baby I had ever seen. I thought it would be wonderful to have a baby sister. It never happened.

In those early years my playmates so often visited my house, that it hardly seemed I was an only child. I can't remember ever being lonely. My mother loved children and she never minded how many were in the house; in fact she encouraged them to come. I can remember my friends and I playing for long hours with dolls and the wooden toys my dad had made for me. Our imaginations knew no limits.

Then came the big adventure: emigration to Canada, a traumatic event for a seven year old only child. Gone were the only friends I had known and the security of my only home. I withdrew into a shell and built a wall around myself. I became a one friend person.

Now I spent many lonely hours and longed for brothers and sisters. I loved to go to homes of friends where there were lots of children and pretended that I belonged there. I wanted to be one of them.

My mother continued to love children and 'adopted' all of the neighbourhood kids, who were much younger than I. She would have parties for any reason so she could invite them all over and have fun with them. I guess she was pretending too.

I can't remember how old I was the year we decided to share Christmas with two little girls from the orphanage. I became caught up in the excitement of buying gifts for them, wondering if they'd like our choices, if they'd feel at home in our house and whether they'd enjoy the dinner. Christmas was wonderful. The girls came again and again that winter and spring, all though Lent, until after Easter, almost every weekend. My parents inquired about adopting them, but it wasn't possible so the relationship stopped. We were all becoming too close.

I spent my high school years at a boarding school in Toronto and loved every minute. There I had so many 'sisters' I could pick and choose my favourites. My tight circle of friends narrowed to four, with a few hangers-on, but again, one became a special friend. Being American, she left after grade 12, and once again I felt a void. But I had my music and through that became close to a newcomer to the school.

My parents had great hopes for me, being their one and only. In many ways I know I failed them, and for many years it was hard for me to live up to their expectations. At the same time I resented being the only child, the one on whom hung all their hopes. I made up my mind that I would not have 'an only child'.

In only the last 25 years or so, since coming into a relationship with Jesus, my older brother, can I look back and give praise to the Father for the way things were. I was a person who resisted authority. I wanted to plan my life for myself.

For example, it was more through my parents' perseverance that I learned to play the piano, but once I had earned my degree, I almost never used my gift. I taught all my own children the basics of music and accompanied them when they sang or played the flute, but that was as far as it went. My father used to beg me sometimes to play for him and for others, and I knew my refusal hurt him, but it was the area of my past that I wanted to put behind me. It was part of me that had been controlled by my parents, and now I was in control.

God, in one of his surprise moves, changed all that. Since my father died, God has built for me a music business, a totally unexpected and unsolicited source of income. The children and adults I teach have all come to me with no effort on my part; never have I advertised or asked for students. From a small beginning, the four children of a friend's family, my group of students has grown tenfold, and I enjoy every aspect of this new career. I sometimes picture my father now sitting up in heaven smiling as he sees me doing what he wished for me all along.

I have been very blessed. My parents were faith-filled people who taught me to love God and to care for others. And God has been faithful, leading me ever deeper into the heart of the Holy Family, awakening and nurturing in me a love for the Church and her teachings.

It's through Pope John Paul II and such writings as *Humanae Vitae* and *Familiaris Consortio* that I have a greater understanding of family. Nowhere is there even an implied expectation that all Catholics are to raise large families, only that they remain generously open to life. Even after we disobey his law, God in his mercy can and does restore that openness which he desires, and marriages that were once sterile bear abundant fruit. Many couples are childless and feel great pain in their barrenness. The Church recognises and empathises with their pain, assures them of her support and affirms them as a family. Many couples have only one or two children;

they are no less a family than those with numerous children.

All life comes with pain. Large families are torn apart for trivial or serious reasons; couples with no children ache to hold a baby of their own; those unable to receive more than one or two children may feel hurt in the presence of large families; the only child feels resentment towards the parents who failed to provide the brothers and sisters. All are family, all part of the broken and wounded family of God, the family of the church.

My family was as much a family as those of my friends who had five, eight or fourteen children. I have asked my parents to forgive me my resentments and the unforgiveness that lay for years unnamed and unclaimed in my storage bin of sin. And I have forgiven my parents for something that my childish understanding saw as their fault, but which I now know was as painful for them as it was for me. I am free now to celebrate my birth family, father, mother, and myself; my own family, husband, wife, three daughters and three sons; and the next generation of family, three sons-in-law and eight grandchildren.

Jesus' life was about showing us how to live, in everything but sin. He experienced everything I have or will ever experience. He was an only child, and he has taught me to rejoice also in being an only child, like him.

Twenty-One

Sleeping in the Barn on Christmas Eve

by Catherine Fournier

It may sound strange, but my husband and I want to sleep in a barn on Christmas Eve. After Christmas Eve Mass, we would rather put the children in the car, drive to a friend's farm and sleep in their hayloft instead of spending the evening dressed in fancy clothes in a decorated home, just to experience for ourselves what the birth place of Jesus was like.

Unfortunately, I can't imagine why, the children aren't as impressed with this idea as we are. For the last three years, they've been yelling 'No, No, No' whenever we try to discuss it. Well, yes, we'd miss the Christmas Eve feast at the grandparents and yes, there'd be no tree with presents in the morning. We could live without that for one year, couldn't we?

'No, *No, No!*'

The only reason we haven't seriously considered this plan yet is that we've always had a little one too young for winter camping. This year, though, Robert will be nearly three. We think it's time.

So Peter and I started talking about it out loud this summer, to test the waters. One day, I asked, 'What happens at Christmas, kids?'

The unanimous answer, 'It's Jesus' birthday and we get presents!'

'So which is more important, Jesus' birthday or presents?'

Again a chorus of voices, 'Jesus' birthday!'

I'm a bit sceptical when I get an answer that easily; it seems too good to be true. So I asked the all important, 'Why?'

'Why is the birthday of Jesus more important than getting toys?'

This time, I received a variety of answers, according to age.

From Jonathon, a shy four, 'Because Jesus was born from God and toys only come from a store'.

From Matthew, our giggly seven, 'Because our toys don't love us'.

From Sarah, an opinionated nine, 'We grow out of our toys or they break, but Jesus lasts forever and always loves us'.

From Andrew, a quiet, perceptive twelve, 'Because presents are only things and Jesus became a person'.

'Well, then, why do we give presents?'

Sarah designated herself as spokesman. 'Because the Wise Men brought presents, and it helps us to make each other happy.'

This still seemed rehearsed, as if they were repeating what they had been taught. So, gradually I brought the subject around to the idea of sleeping in a barn, just like Jesus, Mary and Joseph did.

'Oh, that would be neat! Yeah, it would be just like it was in the olden days. We'd understand about Christmas better, I think', they chorused.

'So, how about doing it on Christmas Eve itself?'

'No, *No*, *No*!'

Later, I spoke with our delightfully blunt fourteen year old about celebrating Christmas. Tina was eight or nine when, as she puts it, 'you guys turned into religious fanatics'. Her childhood memories and understanding of Christmas were formed before we 'changed everything'.

'You know what?' she said, 'I liked Christmas better when I was little, with Santa Claus and all that stuff. It was more fun. I can understand what you're doing now and all, but I miss the old way.'

It may have been more fun for her, but it was rushed and tense for us. The holiday season wasn't a holiday, and the spirit of Christmas was very hard to find.

Our Christmas celebrations once followed the familiar pattern, just like everyone else on the block. A wreath on the front door, a Christmas tree in the living room, evenings of school concerts and parties, culminating in a two day frenzy of driving through snowstorms, present opening and feasting. Christmas Eve with our in-laws, Christmas morning at home, Christmas Mass, then Christmas dinner with my parents, back to the in-laws on Boxing Day.

On Christmas Eve, Peter and I would have to force ourselves to stay awake until our hyped-up kids had gone to sleep so that we could bring out the Santa Claus gifts and fill the stockings. We would hope that they would sleep until at least six o'clock so that we could get enough sleep to cope with the mother-and-adult-daughters-in-kitchen-making-a-turkey-dinner-scene the next day. The next morning it was hard to slow down enough to really pay attention at Christmas Mass, to thank God for the gift he had given to his people in his Son.

We were together as a family in body, but that's about all. Christmas time was always a bit sad because we could tell we were missing something, even though we had no idea of what it was.

The 'changing everything' that Tina referred to started about six years ago when Peter and I began praying regularly and saying evening prayers with the children. We found that regular prayer is like flying in a small airplane. You begin to see things from a different perspective. Familiar objects suddenly have a different orientation.

We became more aware of the distortion of Christmas. It bothered us to realise that we had been taking our children to Mass every Sunday, teaching them their catechism, preparing them for the sacraments, praying together and yet still participating in the secular Christmas routine. We were contradicting ourselves. We had to change.

But children are the original conservatives. Change makes

them high-strung and irrational, prone to wild conclusions and persecution complexes. We knew we'd have to change gradually, one thing at a time, to avoid a mutiny. So we decided to replace each old tradition with a new one, preferably an activity that the children could participate in.

Without any idea of where we were going, we set out to try to make our Christmas more devout and family-centred. It's been an interesting six years.

As a beginning, we built a Jesse tree. A Jesse tree traces the family tree of Jesus through readings from the Old and New Testaments. There is a reading for each day of Advent. A small picture representing each reading is hung on a 'tree'.

We collected branches in the woods, thin ones for the stem and arms and one thick branch to slice for the pictures. I drew outlines of the pictures on one side of the slices of wood with a fine black marker and wrote the reading on the other side. Then, the children painted the pictures with acrylic craft paint, and tied embroidery cotton through small holes drilled through the top. We set the finished tree on a small table in the living room.

Peter and I were surprised by the effect of this simple change. We added the Jesse tree reading to our evening prayers. As Advent went on, the genealogical story drew closer and closer to Christmas morning and the birth of Jesus. The evening readings put a new perspective on Advent and Christmas. We began to realise that Jesus, Mary and Joseph were real people with histories and ancestors.

As the children grew, they took turns with the readings. Often they didn't think the suggested reading was long enough. Especially the story of Joseph and the coat of many colours, 'We can't just leave him there! We have to read on and find out what happens next!' So we continued, travelled to Eygpt, experienced the famine with Joseph's brothers and laughed when they were all reunited.

The next year, we replaced Santa Claus with Saint Nicholas. The feast day of Saint Nicholas is nearly three weeks before Christmas, neatly separating the solemnity of Christmas from the gifts and toys bonanza atmosphere of Santa Claus. An added benefit is that of course Saint Nicholas has never heard of the Ninja Turtles or anything else that's advertised on TV!

A saint in heaven, a good bishop who lived long ago and is now praying for us makes more sense to children anyway, than some strange story about a fat gentleman who comes down chimneys even when there isn't a chimney on the house. You'll never have to grow out of believing in Saint Nicholas either.

We say prayers to Saint Nicholas in the evening and hang our stockings on the backs of the kitchen chairs. Tina and I set and decorate the table before we go to bed. In the morning we have a special breakfast and empty our stockings as we eat. The early morning of 6 December is a pleasant time to relax and enjoy the children's excited chatter without worrying about a turkey, getting to Mass on time or wondering whether stocking gifts are distracting them from the Nativity. Taking Santa Claus out of Christmas, and taking the silly red elf suit off Saint Nicholas has been both the easiest and the hardest of our Christmas changes. On the one hand it is easy because it is a single feast day instead of a daily event like the Jesse tree. In addition, the children enjoy the feast of Saint Nicholas because they get presents before anyone else in their class.

On the other hand, it has been difficult because it doesn't fit what is going on outside the home. Everywhere I go with the children, people ask;

'Have you been a good boy? Are you looking forward to Santa Claus's visit on Christmas Eve?'

At the junior kindergarten Christmas concert last year, in a Catholic school, mind you, the children sang two Christmas carols, and five songs about elves, reindeer, sleigh bells and Santa Claus. It can be confusing, both for the children and for me. They wonder who's telling them the true story, and I wonder how things ever got so far off track.

The year after we restored Saint Nicholas, we introduced an Advent wreath. This has developed into the kind of family-centred activity we were hoping for. The children go out for a walk in the woods with their father and collect evergreen branches for the Advent wreath. Peter helps them find the greenest and bushiest branches. They come back rosy and excited, proud to be helping to celebrate Advent.

I make the wreath by arranging the branches in a bowl filled with wet florist's foam. I carve four holes in the foam to fit the four candles: three purple and one pink. As the year darkens, the Light of God becomes brighter by contrast. To heighten this contrast, we eat dinner only by the light of our Advent wreath. As we get closer to Christmas, the light at the dinner table gets brighter as one more candle is lit each week. Peter and I find the increasing brightness of the Advent wreath complements the growing excitement of the Jesse tree readings, so sometimes we do the reading at the dinner table.

We are pleased by what has happened in our family as a result of the changes we've made. The Jesse tree readings refocus the family's attention every day on the coming of the Christ Child. Our Saint Nicholas Day celebrations separate the excitement of gifts from the excitement of the Birth and allow us to enjoy both more clearly. The Advent wreath gives us all a sense of what the coming of the Light of the World means. We are growing closer together as a family and Christmas time is a happier time for us all.

In the last few years, we've begun to make our Saint Nicholas and Christmas gifts, to shift the emphasis in gift-giving from size and expense to thought and care. With a couple of years of new traditions successfully established, even the most 'conservative' members of the family saw this as a natural next step. We still hear about the classmates who get Nintendo games or new skis for Christmas, but more often in a tone of pity than of envy.

Tina collects grapevines and makes wreaths. Andrew gets busy in the workroom and makes boats and boxes. Sarah draws marvellous pictures and the three smaller boys help me bake cookies and breads. Peter carves small animals out of wood. We've created some traditions in our gift giving as well. Peter and I always give each child a book. We give my brother-in-law and his wife a homemade

Christmas decoration each year. I always give my mother a bell for her collection. We give teachers a jar of jam and a loaf of bread.

Traditions like this keep our gift-giving simple. It helps to remind us that we give gifts to show our love, not to impress the recipient. Homemade gifts take time and thought, which in itself is a better gift than anything with a price tag on it. After all, the gift of the first Christmas was one beyond price. Our family needs to learn now to celebrate the great miracle and gift of Christmas, the birth of a child. The miracle of Christmas is God becoming man in Jesus Christ, bringing salvation and redemption to the world. The gift is that the two are linked together as one of the mysteries of the Church.

The last six years have taught us to look closer at the mystery. We are learning to see how simple and how glorious this mystery is. By stripping away Santa Claus and Jingle Bells, by welcoming true Christmas in, by praying together and working together, we are teaching our children what we learned so slowly ourselves. The best Christmas was the first Christmas, a baby born to poor young parents in a barn. They had no decorated tree, no feast, no presents to give each other, not even a bed for the Baby. But in their poverty and simplicity, they welcomed the Light of Christ and gave Christmas to the world.

The chorus of 'No, No, No!' gets quieter every year.

Twenty-Two

Catechesis and Evangelisation

by Michael O'Brien

Our perceptive eight year old daughter, Elizabeth, once asked me, after a trip to the dinosaur wing of the Natural History Museum, 'Why did God make dinosaurs?'

An excellent question. I glanced hastily about the room wishing that someone would write a book titled, 'How to Answer Children's Unanswerable Theological Questions'. We groped around the matter together for a while, and her questions were really pressing: she wanted to know!

'I mean', she said, 'God is good. But why did he make something so horrible and ugly?'

'Maybe at first he made them to be very big and friendly like whales and elephants', I replied, 'but the devil corrupted the world and changed them from plant-eaters into meat-eaters. Then they started killing . . . ' The answers seemed to ring a little hollow. She knew it and I knew it. I prayed silently. Perhaps it was my guardian angel who prompted a thought:

'Elizabeth, I don't really know for sure, but maybe he wanted to make a creature that looked like something we can't see. Perhaps somewhere in the universe there's an invisible dinosaur on the loose and it doesn't like people.'

She thought about that for a while. After a few minutes she said, 'I get it'.

We nodded together, although there was a little faking in father's nod, because he was still straining to get it for himself.

'Yes', she said, musing, 'maybe God wanted to tell us that it's kind of dangerous here. Like the angels and the devils and all that.'

'Yes, maybe like that.'

'But the dinosaurs weren't evil, were they?'

'No, not at all. They were dangerous, but they weren't bad. Just as a snake or a shark isn't bad. They're creatures. And each of them tells a part of a big story. All of creation is like a book with millions of chapters.'

'Some were scary and some were wonderful.'

'Right! The dinosaurs are gone now, and the world is full of people, but they left a powerful message for us in the fossils, didn't they?'

'Yes', she said, getting really excited. 'And that means we'll never run out of good books to read. There's always a new story.'

Theologians would call this 'a teachable moment'. Family life tends to be full of such moments if one is on the alert for them. But because we parents are often distracted or exhausted by the demands of our times, and because of the temptation in an overly complex environment to shunt the responsibility of catechesis to the trained expert, we may begin to overlook such a moment.

My generation was the last to be raised on the old Baltimore Catechism, that sturdy yeoman of catechesis which accomplished its task of instructing us in the actual content of the Catholic Faith. It taught us doctrine and moral absolutes; though, admittedly, I cannot recall many moments when it imparted the thrill of that Faith I now know to be the greatest adventure of all. As my children arrived at the age of reason and began to ask the great, perennial questions, I began to founder in the gaps left by my own inadequate formation. It was difficult to answer them in ways that helped them to see the connections between truth and their experience. In the ensuing years we have learned through trial and error that their short lives simply do not provide the tools for a complete discernment of reality. In order to understand the meaning and purpose of their lives, they must be equipped with absolutes, with some abstractions, with wisdom. At the same time, vital connections must be made between the realm of ideas and that of lived experience.

My wife and I have searched for a catechesis that would help make these connections, which would retain the doctrinal substance of the old catechisms and enliven its presentation of truth with the new awareness of the role of beauty. It has not been easy to find. We have had to grope our way through a cloud of confusion which covers the intellectual and spiritual climate that has in no small way invaded particular churches. We have found many of the widely-used catechisms to be weak in substance or distorted. A small number, including the exceptional *Faith and Life* series published by Ignatius Press, are most helpful. We have learned to think fast on our feet, to tell stories and use parables and metaphors drawn from the events of each day; we read Scripture and great Catholic novels to our younger children and adolescents; we make time for listening to their questions, talk with them, explain tough theological points to our bright eight year old theologians; we keep growing in devotional life and love of the popes, saints and their teachings; we pray and keep our eyes open, and pray some more; and we trust that the inherent power of the sacraments, the Gospels, and the witness of the sacred arts and the martyrs will be sufficient formation. We worry and suffer and come round again and again to hope. Yet we have learned that we cannot presume upon supernatural rescue operations if the natural ground has not been sufficiently prepared.

Grace builds upon nature, and in order to make a path for grace to do its work the parent must provide a sensitive balance of doctrine and experience, of rite and imagination, of word and image, and above all provide those moments when the child learns to open the doors to the Holy Spirit. The home and the Catholic school must be more than a place where people talk about religious facts or attitudes. They must be houses of prayer. Only in the atmosphere of reverence for being itself will the Holy Spirit be freed to evangelise our children; only in such an environment will catechesis take root. Reverence for being begins within the family. Here, as different personalities are thrust into the tumult of daily household traffic, a thousand encounters take place between soul and soul, person and person. Here, the joyful and the hard sayings of the Gospel 'take on a local habitation and a name'. Here, opportunities abound to crucify one's own selfishness, to feel death and resurrection in one's very flesh. Yes, there's no place quite like home for the transfiguration, or damnation, of man. Our four year old Angela, sweet in temperament, must learn to negotiate with her seven year old brother, Benjamin the Barbarian, whose imagination is only barely baptised. Reflective, critical John, cracking dry theological jokes at the advanced age of eighteen must bear patiently the squabbles of his two 'artistic' sisters, Elizabeth, and fourteen year old Mary. Quiet, gentle, spiritual Joseph aged sixteen, must learn to stand firm against all these stronger wills roaming at large in the household. Mum and Dad, in their mid-forties, somewhat tired out from coping with the stresses of the twentieth century, need the wisdom of Solomon just to get through an ordinary day. Yes, in the Christian home, the human condition is operative full-force. It is this condition that we are called to evangelise and to catechise.

It is tempting to turn catechesis over to the experts. After all, have they not studied the matter in depth? Do they not have so much more energy and maintain order so much more efficiently than most parents, who have their children home from school only for a few tired hours at the end of the workday and on busy week-ends? After all, isn't the Catholic school the Church? Well, yes . . . and no. By which I mean to say that even the most inspired of educational environments is not the complete Church. It is a member, an organ. The family is the fundamental sacred unit, the heart of the *ecclesia*, or in the words of John Paul II, drawing upon the documents of Vatican II, 'the domestic Church'. It bears frequent reminding that if the family is in a state of siege, the Church will be in crisis to its very foundations. No matter what the quality of the 'solutions' applied to the crisis, if there is no hidden, humble, abiding miracle of spiritual regeneration in the culture of the family, even the most masterful catechetical projects will produce little fruit.

A growing number of parents are teaching catechism at home. It is not an easy task. It is not simply a matter of finding the right technique or the best text-book. It is rather a discovery that our inner dispositions either deaden or animate the religious programme. Indeed, parents who have their very selves invested totally can transform a syllabus from information on a page into a living experience for learning the faith. John Paul II has pointed out that in order for Catholic catechesis and religious education to work, teachers' hearts and souls must be shaped by the Spirit of Christ, must think with the mind of the universal Church, must look upon and love their children as part of the flock of Christ. He exhorts us to work for the preservation of a genuine Catholic culture and ecclesiology. He reminds us of the danger of a partial reading of the Council and points out that a unilateral presentation of the Church as a purely institutional structure devoid of her mystery has led to serious deficiencies, especially among the young.

The answer to the many crises of our time is not to be found in applying systemic solutions to the problem of man. Man cannot be saved *from the outside in*, as the informative events of our century have amply proved. The Church knows that collectivist approaches to the human person fail, and always produce at least as much damage as any good they do. The Church is neither collectivist nor individualistic. She is *personalist*, concerned with the salvation of each human person as a unique and mysterious epiphany of the mind of God. Catholic education succeeds to the degree that it is personalist, to the degree that it understands its role as a *subsidiary* support to the home. For in the home, the healthy tensions between the demands of community and the uniqueness of each human soul are experienced to the full. By pouring its efforts into the protection and nurturing of family life, the Church will renew herself from the inside out, and in doing so will minister a long-range healing to society itself. It is a slow method but a sure one.

Autumn Years

Twenty-Three

Making Room at the Inn

by Francis Phillips

Agnes did not celebrate Christmas last year. I did not know it. She was in hospital, in a coma from which she did not wake. All during the time that we were busy giving and receiving gifts, going to and from church, greeting visitors and putting up decorations, she lay unconscious.

I only learned of her illness after the holiday. At the time I was too busy to think of Agnes except at odd moments. I read once that you can only celebrate Christmas if you have religious faith, children or money. Well, we are blessed with the first two, and the bills somehow get paid. But these very blessings can carry the temptation to cocoon oneself against the outside world. When you have a warm room inside the Inn, you might not hear the timid knock of someone outside, asking you for shelter.

Agnes had just such a timid knock, easily muffled by the wind without and the laughter within. Who was she? The answer is, someone I never met and only briefly knew, but whose spiritual presence gradually became a reality in the days and weeks following her death in the small hours of 27 December, the Feast of the Holy Family.

If you edit a paper as I do, you occasionally make a 'pen-friend', someone whose handwriting on the envelope gives you a familiar pleasure and whose letter, you are certain, will always encourage and never cast down. That was how I encountered Agnes.

Out of the blue, she sent a little prayer for our 'Space for Prayer' column. I responded, then she sent a flapjack recipe for the cookery slot. I made them and told her the children were loud in their approval – mine were too dry and crumbly. She then suggested an idea for an article. I thought it a good one and followed it up. Thus our friendship, at first formal and cautious, gradually developed. It had begun only last summer, but soon the wavering calligraphy of her letters became a weekly, and sometimes twice weekly, occurrence. The letters were often very long with several 'P.S.s' scrawled in the margins and even on the envelope itself. Once I received a teabag in the envelope; Agnes wrote saying her letter was so long – it was – that I would need to sit down half way through and drink a cup of tea.

I was always touched, amused, heartened – and intrigued. What was Agnes really like? As time went on and as I pondered the erratic asides in her correspondence, I fitted together bits of the jigsaw. She was unmarried; she lived alone; ill-health had forced her to retire early from work. She only had a small pension. All her time seemed to be spent in the service of others: visiting prisoners, baking cakes for her local hairdresser, praying for priests, particularly seminarians. Only implicitly did I detect a note of suffering behind all this. Although surrounded by loving friends whom she often mentioned to me, Agnes was clearly deeply lonely; the anguish in her heart was not assuaged by the sympathy of others. She did not want to live alone and found it hard to cook for herself. She dreaded the winter, with its cold, dark days, 'grey days' as she described them.

All this I absorbed as the weeks went by. Often I apologised for being in a hurry and only answered her in postcards. It is easy to miss those tentative knocks on the door when you have the role of the innkeeper's wife and many demands are made on your time and energy. Summer turned to autumn and autumn into the dark evenings at the end of the year. In November, Agnes sent me, hesitantly, a piece of writing. She called it a 'meditation' on the fourth mystery of the rosary, hoping it might be suitable for the paper. The meditation centred on those two old people, Simeon and Anna, and the difficulties of old age as it would have appeared to them, with its sense of isolation from, and rejection by, the young and healthy. It was a perspective I had not considered, written simply and from the heart. How much of herself was contained in that meditation, I could only guess. After publication, I received a touching letter of amazement and gratitude; Agnes had a low opinion of herself and was genuinely surprised that I thought she had something worthwhile to say.

After that, her letters suddenly stopped. I sensed something was wrong, but it was December, the school holidays were upon me and then Christmas itself. The Inn was a busy, noisy, excited place, and we had to find room for many visitors. I phoned Agnes' flat a few times but no one answered. Perhaps she was away? Then, just before New Year, I felt compelled to discover the reason for her silence and phoned her old work place – guessed at from the letterhead of one of the odd scraps of paper she used to write on. The voice at the other end said, 'Who are you?'

'A friend', I replied uncertainly.

'Oh, I am so sorry. I have bad news. Agnes died early on 27 December'.

It could not be true. How? Why? Suddenly and acutely, I longed for one of those eccentric diffuse missives. My informant said, 'I'll give you her sister's number. She'll be able to give you more details.'

So I phoned Agnes' sister and described our odd pen-friendship. My voice must have sounded upset for she said gently, 'There was nothing anyone could do. We all tried. She valued her independence but she just wouldn't look after herself. She collapsed in early December and never recovered. She couldn't eat. It was a strange form of anorexia. She weighed less than 90 pounds when she died. God must have wanted it this way; the Holy Family was her favourite feast day and I think she would have liked that to be that day of her death.'

'May I have a photo?' I ventured.

'Of course', was the reply. 'But the best I can give you was taken ten years ago. Agnes wouldn't allow photos in the last few years. Her illness had aged her terribly. Although she was only 56 when she died, she looked much older.'

A few weeks later the photo duly arrived. I saw a tall, handsome woman, well dressed, smiling across a garden, surrounded by golden daffodils. I looked at her face for a long time. How many 'grey days' had followed the taking of that photo? How many attempts to reach out to others, only to return to the silence of her room? How many meals uncooked, or once cooked, left uneaten? How many rosaries prayed in the midst of this suffering, so that young men might remain steadfast to the invitation to follow Christ as celibate priests?

The Feast of the Holy Family. How much had Agnes longed for a family, longed to be loved and cherished at a human hearth? She did not find a place at the Inn. But along with the 'little ones' of this world, the shepherds, the Annas, the Simeons, the lonely and the dispossessed, Agnes was in the place that mattered: the stable, beside the crib with Mary and Joseph, gazing down in wonder at, as she once described him, 'the little King'.

Now, whenever I pray the fourth joyful mystery, Agnes is in my thoughts and her spiritual presence reminds me that I, too, must find room for those who knock at the door of my home, my hearth and my heart.

Twenty-Four

Father and Father-in-Law

by Geraldine Hertz

You may be an exemplary father, and now that the children have grown up strong and healthy, turning out the way you wanted, you may feel that you've got it made. Don't you believe it!

When those wonderful young people leave home, they tend to absorb the loves, hates, desires and conceits of their spouses. At some point a father will have to admit that he's starting all over again. A whole new area of understanding may open up for him, but so may an enlarged breeding place for trouble. A man may suppose his children love him. He may even be very sure of it.

But their spouses can't love him at first glance. How does a father cope with that?

Big sigh. Back to the drawing board to relearn what he's done so well when the children were little: building love. Only this time he may not like the slump of a son-in-law's shoulders or his slouch as he watches TV, or he may just feel jealous that some stranger has carried off his wonderful daughter. He may have to cope with his irritation at a daughter-in-law who he imagines is not good enough for his son, a girl who can't cook and doesn't want to learn, who wants more and more of that elusive thing called 'equality'. No matter how reasonable his feelings may seem, they breed nothing but contempt if left to fester. Remembering that God loves even that young man who seems so unworthy of his daughter, may be of some help. A father-in-law may only be able to love by an act of the will, in the name of God.

But how does a father-in-law *build* love?

It helps if he remembers that he's growing older and that soon the young people will be on their own. It's hard to accept the fact that he's losing this position of dominance. It helps if he can take the time to enjoy those remaining years and trust that his young people will choose spouses who are right for them.

My husband Joe had to adjust to this situation. He was a hot tempered man, finding it easier to be graceful about being a father-in-law when he was a little older. This is how he did it. One Saturday morning, I served coffee to the grown family, many of whom had come visiting with their spouses and their children. Joe, seeing an opportunity to tell stories of the past, leaned back in his recliner and fondled our dog Heinrich's ears as he laughed and spoke about his boyhood years in North Dakota.

'I remember when I was only twelve, and I was disking a large field for my folks. I fell off the disc and it ran over my legs, breaking them above and below the knees and twisting my left foot so that it faced backward. It hurt something fierce as the horses dragged me. I, faced into the dirt, hollering 'Whoooa' until the horses, two big Percheron geldings, stopped.

'I'd have been there all day except that my uncle, from his own house a mile away, noticed that the horses were standing idle for a long time, and he phoned Ma, who got on her saddle horse and came to see what was wrong.

'Well, there was no doctor, so Pa took me to a veterinarian, who couldn't get his licence in this country, and he set my legs. But he set one of them crooked. Later Pa covered the leg with skunk fat and pulled it out straight, breaking it over again and setting it correctly.'

'Gee Grandpa, didn't it hurt?' Daron asked, his eyes round.

'You bet it hurt, but Pa gave me a big swig of whiskey, and then I passed out. Man, that was painful. It was weeks before I could do anything besides sit at Ma's feet and work the treadle of her sewing machine for her with my hands.'

Joe, enjoying the attention of these young people, embroidered the stories so that even the sons-in-law sat down beside him, enthralled.

He knew a captive audience when he saw one, and he expanded as he felt their admiration. His joy would have been complete, except that he noticed the silence of one son-in-law. It occurred to him that this young man was his opposite: a city fellow with a quiet way about him.

My husband's tone shifted to a more serious note. 'None of us is our own man. God made each of us unique, yet all of us are born to live the way he wanted us to!

'As I've lived my way, so you'll find your way. Actually, you remind me of my own father, but he was much shorter, maybe five feet six inches, and slim. It was the way he raised his six sons and six daughters that made me want this kind of family.

'He knew God gave him those kids, and he never failed any of us. He walked with pride, but not in himself, in us! Lots of times we boys liked to coax Pa into playing his harmonica for us while we worked. Boy, did he have rhythm!'

Joe's eyes danced with the memory. 'Of course, it wasn't only his music that kept us straight. Pa had a talent for being there for us in little things. He didn't have to discipline much, because his smile told us when we'd done a good job!'

With eyes softened, Joe added, 'Whenever we walked down the street to church, Pa smiled and nodded at people, and everyone smiled back! I don't know how he did that, but everyone loved him. Even his enemies liked to joke with him.'

Joe looked up, and his eyes locked with those of our son-in-law. 'Son', he said, 'you remind me of my pa. You're quiet, like him, and that's good. Sometimes, I talk too much.'

Everyone noticed how Joe had shifted the emphasis from himself to the young man, and in that moment, I suddenly knew why Joe was loved just as his father had been loved. I don't think he knew how much of his own father had gone with him into his adult life. But we did. Our daughters still talk about the joy of being picked up by Daddy and danced around the kitchen on a Sunday morning, to the schottisches and polkas that rocked our kitchen in those days. His sons and daughters still look at their photo albums years later, and proudly point out for their own kids how many ways they are like their beloved Grandpa!

Joe had discovered a priceless secret that is even more needed today. He'd learned that the greatest thing a father can do is to love his family as Christ loves his Church; that if he can do that, his love can change the world.

Fathers and fathers-in-law, getting along with your married children and their spouses is quite easy, once you've figured it out. The key word is *enjoy*! If you pray to God for patience and you treat each person who comes near you with the love God meant all Christians to have for one another, then enjoyment is a natural result. Have fun with them. Share with them what you know. Listen to their problems, of course, but don't let them burden you unduly. Pass those troubles on to God, who can do something about them. Your own love and your hard-earned understanding will come full circle. A circle that sends its ripples outward in ever widening rings until your devotion encompasses and enriches all who know you.

Twenty-Five

Still Bearing Fruit

by Paul Lissandrello

My grandmother taught me how to pray. She never gave me any formal instruction. She taught by example. Grandmother prayed simply and faithfully every day. Her commitment showed her grandchildren that prayer was a very important part of life. When my five brothers, sister and I were children, we always looked forward to Grandmother Mary's regular visits. She always brought good things to eat, and took over in the kitchen to prepare delicious Italian meals for us.

Sunday afternoon dinner with Grandmother Mary always seemed to be a big feast. It would typically consist of soup, a pasta dish, roasted chicken and the finishing touches of pastries she acquired from our favourite Italian bakery. My mother helped her in the kitchen, eventually taking over most of the work as grandma's health began to fail.

Grandmother Mary had diabetes which, over a period of time, became progressively worse. Being of the 'old world', she didn't like to go to doctors and, by the time she did, her condition was not reversible.

Our family sadly watched as she got weaker and lost the ability to cook her wonderful meals we were used to. I'll never forget her breaking into tears when a special Sicilian rice dish she was making, one of our favourites, turned out to be a 'disaster', or so she thought. We couldn't convince her that, although it didn't look the way it was supposed to, it was still delicious.

The ability to cook was an important part of who my grandmother was and, when she had to step back and leave all the food preparation and kitchen work to my mother, she had a very real sense of being useless. However, in spite of her loss of ability in the kitchen, she never lost her ability to pray. Perhaps she prayed as well as she cooked.

Whenever she stayed at our house, which was often, Grandmother rose before anyone else and sat in the living room with her little black prayer book, so old and worn that the binding had to be replaced with cloth. Memorial cards commemorating relatives and friends who died before her, including her husband, filled the pages of the well-used book.

As children growing up, we came down to the living room on Saturday mornings to watch cartoons and to see Grandma in a stuffed chair, her feet on a footstool to help her circulation, prayer book on her lap. She never let our cartoons interrupt her prayer book readings.

Her beads seemed mysterious to us because they had a heavy crucifix containing specks of sand from the Holy Land.

She whispered her prayers in Italian, so low that we could barely hear them, but the sound of her praying would sometimes annoy us because we wanted to hear our cartoons without distraction.

Nevertheless, her faithfulness in praying fervently each day helped us to realise that prayer is an important part of life, something you do every day. We also learned that it doesn't matter how young or old you are, you should pray, as you are able, throughout your life.

As our grandmother grew older, she had more time to pray for the increasing number of her deceased relatives and friends. After all, she was no longer busy in the kitchen. If she couldn't cook for others, she could at least pray for others.

In her last months of life, she had considerable pain with her illness and I believe that she accepted this in a redemptive way, not resenting her condition but sanctifying it by offering it to God. Her prayers and suffering made her far from useless. She was useful to

God, to her family, living and dead, for whom she prayed, and to the Church as a whole, for whom she also prayed. Every morning and evening, as she eagerly invoked the Holy Trinity, the Mother of God and her favourite saints, she knew in her heart that her prayers were being heard.

Since those early days of my youth, when I observed my grandmother praying in the stuffed chair in our living room, prayer has continued to play an important role in my life. I have read many articles and books about the subject and have listened to inspiring talks and homilies. However, one of the most eloquent witnesses to the value of prayer in my experience is the memory of my grandmother's simple, steady and faithful practice.

My wife, Pat, was also influenced by the praying of a grandparent, but in her case, it was her grandfather, Patrick, the son of immigrants from Galway, Ireland. He, too, demonstrated the qualities of simplicity, steadiness and faithfulness in his connection with God.

A man successful in his family life and at work, providing generously for all who were dependent on him, he maintained from his youth a deep spiritual sense that kept him aware of always being in God's presence. His piety was also uncomplicated, centred around an unquestioning love of the sacraments, especially the Eucharist, and popular devotions, such as the rosary and novenas to the Blessed Virgin Mary and various saints.

I have very fond memories of taking him, a man in his mid-80s, to the Montfort Fathers' shrine of Our Lady of the Island in Eastport, Long Island. Bowed down with age and perpetually saddened by the loss of his wife of many years, he regained a certain vitality whenever we went to this holy place. He seemed to be eager to be there and absorbed by every moment, genuflecting, lighting candles and prayerfully moving his lips. Once, as we sat together in a pew near the altar of the shrine chapel, the priest dropped the metal cover to the ciborium which contains the consecrated hosts. Grandpa sprang from his seat and quickly bent down to retrieve the ciborium cover for the priest. His spontaneous act was itself a kind of prayer, a loving action directed toward God in generosity, faithfulness and love. I know that this type of behaviour inspired my wife, her sister and brother when they were young.

This devotion that my wife's grandfather demonstrated in his old age reminds me of a passage in Psalm 92, which refers to God's elderly as, 'still bearing fruit when they are old, still full of sap, still green, to proclaim that the Lord is just'.

I know that the role of grandparent is probably not too far ahead in my future and it is something I am looking forward to. I pray that when I am elderly and not much use for worldly pursuits, I will still have that spiritual 'sap', that holy 'greenness', that faithful fruitfulness which will be pleasing to God and hopefully influence my own grandchildren.

Perhaps another psalm best expresses my situation:

'God, you taught me when I was young,
and I am still proclaiming your marvels.
'Now that I am old and grey, God, do not desert me;
let me live to tell the rising generation
    about your strength and power,
about your heavenly righteousness.'

Psalm 71:17-18.

Isn't this the true vocation of the elderly, to use the abundance of time they have, not only to become closer to God in prayer, but also to teach the 'rising generation', their grandchildren, about our marvellous God and how to relate to him? When they do this, they will be far from useless; they will still bear fruit.

Twenty-Six

The Miraculous Medal and Me

by Ed Billet

On May 2, 1806, Pierre Labouré and Madeleine Gontard were blessed with their sixth child. The Labourés' were wealthy farmers who lived in the small village of Fain-les-Moutiers in Burgundy. The birth of a child was not an extraordinary event in nineteenth century Europe, where births were plentiful and infant deaths high. Madeleine Gontard had borne seventeen children before she died at the age of 52. Six had died prematurely.

The birth of little Catherine was not seen as a special event, even though the church bells rang the Angelus at her birth. Nobody knew that God had great plans for her.

Catherine was nine years old when her mother died. Following her initial grief, she chose the Blessed Virgin for her mother. Catherine received first Holy Communion three years later, after which she became 'entirely mystic', to quote her younger sister Tonine. At age eighteen she had her first premonitory dream that laid the foundation for her vocation. But despite her mystical disposition, her life was governed by reason. From age twelve, until she entered the Vincentian Order of the Sisters of Charity twelve years later, she ran the family household, consisting of five family members and twelve farm hands.

Soon after she entered the Vincentian Order, she began to have visions. They climaxed in three apparitions of the Blessed Virgin, which led to the creation of what today is known as the Miraculous Medal. On Saturday, November 17, 1830, the sisters were gathered in the chapel for their evening meditation. Suddenly Catherine saw Mary, Queen of Heaven. Church archives describe the vision as follows: 'the Virgin's clothes had the whiteness of dawn and in her hands she held a golden ball. As the ball vanished from her hands, her arms swept with a gesture of compassion, while from her fingers rays of light streamed upon a white globe at her feet. An oval frame of letters formed around the image and Catherine could read the words: 'O Mary, conceived without sin, pray for us who have recourse to thee.' Then a voice spoke: 'Have a medal struck after this model. All should wear it around the neck. Grace will abound for those who wear it with confidence.'

Catherine then was shown the reverse of the medal. It contained a large M surrounded by a bar and a cross. Beneath the M were the hearts of Jesus and Mary, the one crowned with thorns, the other pierced with a sword. Twelve stars encircled the whole. The vision disappeared.

*   *   *

After the sudden death of my father when I was eight, we moved from London, England, to my mother's birth place, a small German village located near the Dutch-Belgian border. I received first Holy Communion there two years later and soon became an altar boy. Rural life was closely linked to the Church calendar, and as my childhood years began to revolve around the various feasts and rituals of the Church, I gradually lost a certain feeling of alienation and found my way into the village community. The splendour of liturgical ceremonies became my refuge from cultural shock and later from the effects of poverty, after we lost most of our savings during the depression of the 1920s.

As the days grew longer during Lent and we walked the Stations of the Cross during evening devotions, I experienced feelings of anticipation and dreamed of Easter and the glories of spring. Lent climaxed when the church bells became silent on Holy Thursday. They did not ring again until the Gloria was sung at the Easter Vigil. During this period of silence we altar boys walked through the village, summoning the congregation to church with wooden clappers,

I recall the month of May and its Marian devotions. It was a time when we brought spring flowers to the statue of Our Lady that adorned our small house altar. Church bells merged with the sounds of the village band when a solemn procession wound its way through the village on the feast of Corpus Christi. Walking under a gold-embroidered canopy on a carpet of spring flowers, the priest carried the Blessed Sacrament, stopping for solemn blessings at the four altars that had been erected along the road. The air was heavy with the smell of incense and the fragrance of spring. During the summers we anxiously awaited the annual parish pilgrimage to a Marian shrine, about a six hour walk away. The idyllic little town that harboured the shrine was nestled in a deep valley within the Eifel Mountains.

Our lives changed when Hitler came to power. Life began to move at an alarming pace. Individual freedom was exchanged for an affluence that stifled our souls. The cacophony of blaring brass, the stomping of jack-boots on city pavements, the Teutonic arrogance of Hitler's followers, held everyone at bay. Since my mother was known to have spent many years outside her country of birth, had married a Frenchman and had her son and daughter registered as British subjects, she was immediately under surveillance. But when the Nazis began frantically to prepare for war in Europe and seized anyone fit for military duty, I was drafted into their army at age 22. We had the choice of leaving the country or my sister and I becoming German citizens. We chose the latter.

In the summer of 1940, I saw my mother for the last time. Her tiny figure looked frail and her face bore the evidence of constant pain. A deteriorating disease of the spine had gradually disabled her and confined her to a wheelchair. My unit was about to be transferred to south-eastern Europe.

'I want you to wear this medal. If you say three Hail Marys every day, to which you add: "O Mary, conceived without sin, pray for us who have recourse to thee", I am sure that the Blessed Virgin will protect and guide you safely through this dreadful war.'

My mother then carefully sewed a medal of the Immaculate Conception, also known as the Miraculous Medal, into the leather pouch that we wore around the neck, the pouch containing a disc with our identity number. I promised to wear the medal, but seldom spoke the prayers that were attached to it. My faith was no longer the centre of my life, as it had been during my childhood and early adolescence.

In late 1940, German troops occupied Romania and Bulgaria. In the early morning hours of April 6, 1941, we invaded Greece. As our guns pounded the country's heavily fortified northern borders, I suddenly realised it was Palm Sunday, the day the Church remembers how Christ triumphantly entered the Holy City. I saw the terrible irony of my circumstances. Did I pray? I can't remember. But I know that from this moment on my life was repeatedly saved by what I used to call 'lucky breaks'. While many could be explained away by the laws of cause and effect, a few of them in particular remain enigmatic.

It happened during our long thrust toward Athens, when we drove along the narrow winding roads of the Macedonian mountains without rest or sleep. I was sitting beside the driver of our gun carriage with my eyes closed, when I suddenly felt somebody shaking me. I had just enough time to grab the steering wheel and prevent our crew of six from plunging into the depths of the valley hundreds of feet below. Our driver had fallen asleep. Nobody from the crew could have touched me, as they were riding in the rear of the vehicle.

We reached Athens on April 21, and four weeks later, German airborne units attacked the Mediterranean isle of Crete. Despite heavy losses, the airfield was captured after a day of savage fighting. Our unit landed the next day on a narrow strip of runway amidst crushed gliders and burning planes. During the next five days, about 6000 Germans died during the Battle of Crete; 4,460 are buried on a hill overlooking the airfield. Although often close to death, I survived the battle unhurt.

We remained on the island until early December 1941. I received regular mail from home in which my mother told me about the constant prayers she said for my survival. She was convinced that through the intercession of our Blessed Mother I would continue to be saved, and she urged me not to forget to pray.

On December 3, our unit was sent home on leave and then to the Russian front. That is, except for four men, who were to accompany our anti-tank guns to North Africa and act as instructors. I was one of them. At a later date my mother wrote to me that one of my former superiors had visited her. He told her that our unit had been literally wiped out in Russia.

I arrived in Africa during Rommel's first retreat, and in days my new unit was outnumbered by enemy forces and surrendered. I recall riding on the trails of my anti-tank gun tied in a makeshift way to a truck. Suddenly, we came under attack. A bullet grazed my neck, and I jumped to safety. Seconds later, our truck driver was hit and the truck turned over.

I spent Christmas in an internment camp near Tobruk, Egypt. Here I served Mass once more, received the sacraments, felt the peace of God's presence and resigned myself to his will.

But as we were moved from transit camp to transit camp, from Egypt to Palestine, from Suez to the Union of South Africa, I felt the pressure of being caged in. A young paratrooper and I decided to escape. As we both were fluent in English, we chose to wear British uniforms, tailored from our German khaki great coats.

In the spring of 1942, we were taken by ship from a transit camp near Durban, South Africa, to the Cape of Good Hope. Here we met a number of other vessels, all carrying prisoners of war destined to board the Queen Elizabeth for Canada. Our ship was anchored less than a mile from shore. At nightfall we tied hammocks together to form a rope, which we tied to one of the bunks. We opened one of the portholes, lowered the rope and squeezed ourselves through the opening. My companion reached the ocean safely, but when I was about halfway down, the hammocks came apart, and I hit the icy water with a loud splash. As the guards on deck fired aimlessly at us, a patrol boat came racing to the scene. Pulling us out, one of the patrollers said, 'You guys must be crazy. Don't you know that the waters here are teeming with sharks?'

I spent four and a half years as a prisoner of war in Canada. In early 1942, my mother received word that I was missing in action. After three months of almost unbearable uncertainty, she learned the truth. The burden of insecurity added to her physical suffering, and she slowly pined away. Her letters, however, were testimony of her unshakable faith and her resignation to God's will. Time and again, she assured me of her constant prayers and encouraged me to thank God and his Blessed Mother for having survived the perils of war. Up to her last letter, when her fine handwriting had changed to an almost unintelligible scribble, her spirit remained unbroken, although she had suffered a stroke. She died the following day at age 64.

After my mother's death, I began to realise the effect the Miraculous Medal had had on my life, especially during times of great danger. While my mother was still alive, I had attributed my safety, what I soon recognised as divine intervention, to her incessant and fervent prayers. But after her death strange coincidences kept protecting me and shaping my life. One incident remains unforgettable. I was sent back to Germany in 1948, married in 1949, and my wife and I emigrated to Canada in the summer of 1951. The following year we decided to visit Gravenhurst, a town about 120 kilometres north of Toronto. I had spent part of my incarceration there. I drove, with my friend in the passenger's seat while our wives occupied the back seats. We were just beyond Toronto, travelling on a narrow highway, when we ran into a thunder storm.

As the windscreen wiper fought a futile battle with pouring rain, I was suddenly blinded by the glare of an oncoming vehicle. A split second later we felt a crushing blow, and before we realised what had happened, our car had been thrown into a roadside ditch. The driver's side crumpled and partially ripped from the chassis. The vehicle was a complete write-off. The other vehicle, a huge transport truck, had landed on the opposite side of the road with a blown tyre. Miraculously, the only injury was a slight cut on my friend's forehead.

*   *   *

On June 30, 1832, nearly two years after Catherine's vision, the first 2000 medals were delivered to Fr Aladel, Catherine's confessor. From 1832 to 1836, a total of ten million medals were distributed throughout the world. Before long, the medal became so famous for the graces that were granted through its pious use that it was given the name the Miraculous Medal. At her request, Catherine remained unknown to the world, and even remained anonymous within her own community for 46 years. She told the other sisters about the vision shortly before her death at age 70. Catherine was canonised on July 27, 1947. Her body, exhumed in 1933 and found to be totally incorrupt, lies in the chapel of the motherhouse at 140 Rue du Bac, Paris, beneath the statue of the Virgin of the Globe. There it is venerated by thousands of pilgrims each year. Many miraculous healings have occurred at the site. Countless individuals wearing the Miraculous Medal were, and still are, touched by God's grace through the intercession of the Blessed Virgin. I am one of them.

Twenty-Seven

Five Little Souls in Heaven

by Ellie Hrkach

From the time I was very young I wanted to have a large family. At nine years old, I had ten little dolls with names and personalities. I pretended I was grown-up and had ten children. As a teenager, I dreamed of a large family. When I first met my husband, James, one of the most important questions I asked was, 'How many children do you think you'd like to have?' His answer was a typical James answer, 'I don't know. Four or five, I guess.'

So when we decided to plan our first pregnancy several years later, we were thrilled to think we could possibly be creating a new life and impatiently waited to see if I would miss my period. I never expected any problems since I had never used any form of artificial birth control, we use and teach Natural Family Planning, I never had any sexually transmitted diseases and was basically healthy.

Two weeks after we actively sought a pregnancy, my temperature was still elevated and no period came. We were ecstatic, though a bit scared to think we would be parents. I had waited a long time to actually have a baby and now my dream seemed to be coming true. Three days later, I started to bleed. 'Oh, no', I moaned, 'this can't be happening'.

The doctor dismissed my concern; the bleeding was probably my period.

I knew differently. 'I've got eighteen days of elevated temperatures, and the temperature is not going down.' Patronisingly, the doctor told me not to worry.

I couldn't be convinced; something was wrong. By now, the pregnancy test was positive, and I still bled. Several more doctors confirmed my bleeding as a miscarriage, 'If it's going to happen, it's going to happen'.

The diagnosis still didn't seem right. I finally approached a young intern who listened, looked at my NFP charts and sent me to a specialist. Several days later, I entered the hospital for surgery to remove an ectopic pregnancy from my right Fallopian tube, while leaving the tube in place. An ectopic pregnancy occurs when the baby implants somewhere other than the uterus and has no chance for survival. 'It's funny', said the anaesthesiologist. 'You had placental tissue in the uterus which means you had a baby there too, which miscarried.' I didn't think find it funny. Two babies, lost.

Though my life had been spared, I felt emptiness for the children I would never know. The little soul taken from my tube had a beating heart, a perfect baby. Did I do something wrong by having that operation? These questions were answered by a priest who was also a good friend. He assured me that the removal of an ectopic pregnancy was not morally wrong because that baby cannot grow and survive in the tube. Furthermore, if the baby had not been removed, I would probably have died.

As well as the grief and guilt I experienced another emotion: uncertainty. The surgeon told me I might not be able to have children. Women who have had ectopic pregnancies tend to have more of them. 'But one baby did make it to the uterus', I said. That gave me a measure of hope.

While in the hospital, I prayed and reflected on what had happened. I wanted so desperately to be a mother. In prayer, I implored God to baptise the two little souls that I had conceived and carried for a short time. I prayed that God would someday bless us with more children.

Several months later, we tried again for a pregnancy and prayed that God would bless us with a baby. No period came that month, my temperature remained elevated and I started to have morning sickness. Thrilled, James and I prayed that the baby would be in the right spot. Three weeks later, the ultrasound confirmed that the baby was in the uterus and growing normally.

When our son, Joshua, was born nearly six and a half years ago, James and I cried with joy. I was a mom and he was a dad, and we had a beautiful baby, certain he would be the perfect baby of our dreams. Joshua, however, was to be one of the biggest challenges we have ever faced. For the first three months he did little but cry – scream is a more appropriate word. He slept no more than 20 minutes at a time until nearly six months old. He had screaming fits that lasted for hours into the night. No, Joshua was not that perfect baby I had dreamed about, but, more importantly, he was a baby who needed our love and affection.

A year and a half later, we became pregnant again. Benjamin, born in September 1989, caused me very little morning sickness and was a quiet, sleepy baby who nursed every four hours and slept long periods at night. With Benjamin, we tried to avoid answering 'Yes!' too quickly whenever anyone asked, 'Is he a good baby?'

When Ben was eighteen months old, we became pregnant a fourth time. With two normal pregnancies carried to term, I was confident this would be the same. Seven weeks into the pregnancy, I suffered a miscarriage. Again, we grieved.

At this point, we had conceived five babies in four pregnancies: one tubal pregnancy, two miscarriages and two live births. Though I had two beautiful little boys, I still felt a strong desire to have more children. Three months later, I again conceived. I knew from the beginning that this wasn't a normal pregnancy. My temperature was moderately high, but I began bleeding at the outset. My first thought was, 'Oh God, please don't ask me to give up another baby'. The doctors informed me that I had another ectopic pregnancy; the baby probably died on its own and was expelled naturally.

During this short fifth pregnancy, I neglected my prayer life. I refused what God asked. I denied what happened. At times, I even neglected Josh and Ben. I was depressed for weeks. Women with newborns or pregnant women caused my eyes to fill with tears.

My depression turned to anger. 'It's not fair. I want more children and I may not be able to have more.' I felt angry at people who sterilised themselves, who threw God's gift of fertility away. I felt angry at God, and I was not an easy person to live with.

Sensitive and understanding for the most part, James slowly lost patience with me. One night after the boys were in bed, he sat me down and said, 'We need to talk'. He tried to help me see the problem. 'Ellie, I think you need to focus on God, not on yourself. We need to start praying more.' He reminded me that being open to God's will meant being open not only to having a large family, but to also having a small family, if that was what God had planned. It seemed to me that perhaps I had been trying to choose what I thought God should plan for me, instead of seeking and accepting his actual will.

During this time we had been actively trying for a pregnancy and each month I had my period. Several months went by, and I began to accept that perhaps we might not have any more children. Then, once again, we became pregnant. I now had two small children, ages four and two, to care for and I was sick much of the time with nausea and migraine headaches. I began to realise that God wasn't just giving in to what I wanted; he was asking me to suffer. And yet, in the end, it *was* what I wanted.

Seven months later, I gave birth to our third son, Timothy. We rejoiced and welcomed him into our family. When Timmy was 10 months old, I started to experience some signs of fertility. Because I was still breast feeding quite a bit, and he had only just started on solids, I fully expected to have a period several days later. No period came. Since I hadn't been taking my temperature, I bought an at-home pregnancy test, and it showed positive. I was shocked. But I felt confident that since God seemed to go out of his way to create this baby, it had to be a normal pregnancy.

I was scheduled for an ultrasound a short while later. Before the ultrasound, I prayed and said, 'Lord, you know I want this baby to be in the right spot. But whatever you decide, I'll joyfully accept.' The ultrasound showed no pregnancy sack within the uterus and it turned out to be another ectopic pregnancy in the right tube.

While in the operating room being prepared for surgery, one of the nurses came over to me and asked, 'Is there anything I can do for you?' I replied, 'Yes, there is something you can do for me. I was wondering if you would baptise my baby when the doctor removes it from the tube.'

She looked surprised and then smiled and said, 'I would love to do that for you'. After the surgery, she thanked me; she had never been asked to do something like that.

I spent four days in the hospital. James brought Josh, Ben and Timmy to see me every day. It was quite apparent that Timmy missed Mommy the most. Up until that time, I had never left him for more than an hour or two. Also, he still nursed, especially at night, and he cried a lot of the time because I could not be there for him, which was one of the most difficult aspects of the whole experience.

While I was in the hospital, the doctor recommended that I have my right tube removed since we had had two confirmed ectopic pregnancies in that tube. He explained that he had originally left the tube in place because of our desire to have more children. However, he said that it would probably be in our best interests to have that tube removed since it obviously malfunctioned, though he admitted the tube had no scarring and appeared normal.

We didn't know what to think. On the one hand, the doctor made sense. Having that tube removed might increase our chances of conceiving a normal pregnancy. On the other hand, perhaps we weren't trusting God enough. Confused, we prayed and asked God to help guide in our decision. As it turned out, God saved us from making the choice.

Two weeks after surgery for the ectopic pregnancy, I experienced severe pain in the area where the right tubal pregnancy had been. I knew the physical pain of childbirth, abdominal surgery, miscarriage and ectopic pregnancy, but I had never felt anything like this before. I vomited and nearly fainted from the intense pain.

In the emergency room, I laid on the stretcher, shivering. The nurse gently laid a warm blanket on me. 'Thanks, but I'm not cold', I said. 'I guess I'm scared.' I started to cry, and more importantly, to pray. 'God, I don't want to die and leave my little boys without a mother. Please give me the courage to get through this. If it's your will that I die, please give my family the courage to get through it as well.' I stopped shaking and physically felt God's presence around my body, protecting me.

Just then a kind-looking surgeon asked, 'So what's the problem?' I briefly explained. He responded, 'How many pregnancies have you had?' My answer was almost comical. 'Seven pregnancies and eight babies: three ectopic pregnancies, two miscarriages and three live births.'

After being examined by the doctor, I was diagnosed as having trophoblastic, or foetal tissue still growing in the tube, even though the baby had been removed. The hospital scheduled me for emergency surgery.

During surgery, it was found that the right tube was the size of a large dill pickle. In a normal pregnancy, the trophoblastic tissue is the outer portion of the embryo which is as invasive as cancer and helps the embryo implant in the uterine wall. When it exists without a pregnancy, it is still like cancer. In less than two weeks, it grew from microscopic tissue to the size of several large tumours inside the tube, all over the ovary and all over the bowel.

After the surgery, the surgeon said, 'You were right to come in when you did. You would have had literally seconds to live if it had exploded.'

When I think of the babies that we have lost, I am saddened that I never got to hold, cuddle or nurse them. But as a well-known Catholic speaker has said, 'It is our job as parents to help our children to heaven. When we lose a baby through miscarriage, we have done our job and our child is in heaven.' I believe James and I have five little souls in heaven.

I remember questioning God after my first pregnancy. 'Why did you allow this to happen when you knew these babies wouldn't be born?' I now realise that God created all those little souls for a reason: they have eternal life. I consider it a privilege and honour to have helped to create life and to have carried those babies even for a short time.

I now know a tiny portion of what Mary must have felt to carry Jesus for nine months, nurture and love him for 33 years, only to have him suffer and die in front of her. She accepted all this without question and without doubt. Any suffering I experience or have experienced has caused me to feel closer to Christ. I no longer ask God to take away worry that perhaps we will not be able to have more children or that perhaps I'll have another ectopic pregnancy. I am learning to trust God completely.

Twenty-Eight

New Life

by Abigail Hearth

From a young age I felt that family was one of the highest values, and I looked forward to getting married and having children. After high school, I travelled to Jerusalem to study Judaism and to figure out God's plan for me. 'Please show me your will for me. I'll do anything for you, just guide my path', I prayed. Without any distinct instruction, I decided that marriage and children was the best way I could serve God. In marriage I could be self-sacrificing, loving and grow spiritually.

At the age of nineteen, I married and had a child. Another child was born two years later and a third child two years after that. Two of the children were born at home; I was very committed to our health and doing things as naturally as possible. I thought this was one way I could honour God's sovereignty and his creation.

When I learned in grade 8 that a woman is born with all her eggs and that anything we ingest that harms our bodies would also harm our egg supply, I decided then and there to avoid drugs, alcohol, and cigarettes and maintain a healthy diet. I have always looked to the well-being of my children even before they were born.

Thus when I was married, I wanted to use a natural form of birth control. I attended a course on the Sympto-Thermal Method of Natural Family Planning at the Catholic Information Centre, although I had no idea or curiosity about what Catholicism represented. I was also adamantly opposed to abortion and became involved in the fight against abortion. Abortion indicated to me society's lack of devotion and homage to God and the gift of life.

Meanwhile, my marriage crumbled. In 1983, the five of us took the bus to Edmonton to spend Christmas with my husband's grandmother. On Boxing Day, I woke up feeling sick, pregnant. For Natural Family Planning to work, a couple has to co-operate and be 100% committed to the plan. I didn't have the full support of my husband. A pregnancy test revealed that I was in fact pregnant, so I flew home with my one year old, and consulted my doctor.

Now on my third unplanned pregnancy out of four, my doctor knew of my tenuous relationship with my husband. We had already split up and re-united twice. She advised me to have the child and then have my tubes tied.

Returning to our home in the Gulf Islands, I found my husband stressed and angry with me. I felt I had no choice but to leave, and this would be for the last time.

A single parent, 25 years old, sick and pregnant with no home and no income, it was hard to imagine a future without my husband to whom I was deeply attached, and give up on my 'best dream', the dream of living my life out with one special person whom I cared for in sickness and in health, for better or worse, till death did us part. For three years I lived in denial, hopeful that we would be reconciled. For four years after that I suffered as I truly let go, and still it is hard.

As a pregnant young mother of children aged one, three and five, I sought the advice of family, friends, doctors and my Rabbi and his wife. How would I care for my children when pregnancy makes me so incapacitated with illness? I was led to believe that I really didn't have a choice: abortion. I don't remember feeling any emotional response; I had either steeled myself or I was numb. I had the abortion, and because I knew I had sinned against God, I went back to the hospital a few months later and underwent sterilisation. In my mind that was the price a woman should pay for making such a profound mistake; she must give up the privilege of fertility.

Over the past thirteen years, I have faced the consequences

and my shame, guilt and grief. I am angry with society for the minimisation of abortion and its ramifications. I am angry that I wasn't offered counselling before or after the abortion, and that I wasn't offered alternatives. This society which so highly insists on disposing anything not considered useful, made it easy and cheap to throw away not only a life, but my fertility. This second sin, sterilisation, also had many harmful effects. Since I was closed to having more children, sex could be engaged in without commitment. I became cynical about sex because, deep down, I still felt sex was sacred in spite of my experiences.

I have suffered deeply from depression and anxiety in the past ten years. In my pain I reached out to Jesus, to God who understands suffering. I was baptised a Christian in 1993 and I became a Catholic in 1994. My marriage was annulled the same year. I feel I have come home. I have found my spiritual family, a family that shares my love for God, and sees the sacredness of sexuality, marriage, children and life. I have felt no condemnation from the Church, but compassion.

My children are now fourteen, sixteen and eighteen; the youngest lives in heaven. They are a wonderful blessing in my life and we love each other very much. Last summer I had my tubes untied. Unlike the operation for sterilisation which was free on the medical plan and easy to get, the operation to restore fertility cost three thousand dollars, took three hours and one hundred stitches. This operation was an important step in my healing process.

When I arrived home from the hospital a few hours after surgery, I found a package waiting for me. Opening it, I found a large, colourful banner of Our Lady of Guadalupe, patroness of the unborn. A girlfriend had suddenly sent it to me; she had no idea of what the picture represented. She is Jewish and didn't know I was having the operation. It was a lovely 'coincidence' that affirmed for me that God shows he cares in countless ways. After much thought and prayer, I was finally able to join the Life Chain this year, carrying my own sign: 'Don't Make My Mistake'. This healing has been fostered by a friendship with a man I met at my church. A lifelong Catholic, he has always considered marriage, sexuality and life sacred. His example has encouraged me to let go of my cynicism and reclaim my values. I thank God for the new life he has given me in Christ.

Twenty-Nine

Rosepetal

by Mariea Hall

I always thought that a miscarriage would not be terribly emotionally upsetting.

I am certainly pro-life and have even worked professionally in the pro-life movement in the United States before God gave me a family of my own. I know the facts of life, and I understand that it begins at conception. As a mother, I accept my much-prayed-for little ones as family just as soon as I have any inkling they are there.

But the truth is that we co-exist uneasily for the first several months. I am physically exhausted and sick. I pray, 'O Lord, I am barely coping as it is. How can I function with less energy and more work to do?' I contemplate with ambivalence the end of pregnancy, the suffering of labour followed by the joy of at last seeing my dear one face to face. And then the exhaustion of caring for a newborn.

Throughout my pregnancies, maternity has dawned only slowly. So I always assumed that if I had a miscarriage it would not be too traumatic, robbing me, as it were, of a gift that I had not yet begun to fully appreciate.

And I was right, or so it seemed. As the spotting of the early days gave way to heavier bleeding, I resigned myself to losing the baby we had been asking God to give us for nearly a year. On the Feast of the Holy Innocents, I rose, still bleeding, but also feeling my usual pregnancy exhaustion. By noon, though, the pregnancy 'feeling' was completely gone. I felt fine, even energetic. The headache I'd had for the last month and a half had disappeared and I had no trace of nausea. I just didn't feel pregnant at all. A phone call to my doctor's office confirmed what I feared and informed me which warning signs would require medical attention. In response to my questions, the doctor assured me with all pontifical certainty that I should not worry about baptism, nor about trying to recognise my baby's remains.

I felt a loss, but no grief. I reflected briefly on the Holy Innocents, senselessly slaughtered, yet in some way also giving their lives for a lofty cause, the protection of our infant Redeemer. What was the reason for my baby's death? What was the reason for its life?

I could not answer these questions, so I turned my attention to another matter. I prayed that I would find the baby's remains and not send them down the sewer. I was able to contact a Catholic obstetrician in another state who understood my priorities, gave me the details I needed to know and explained conditional baptism under these circumstances. He also strongly urged me to bury the baby's remains on consecrated ground and to name the poor little one.

Name the baby? I had not considered it. We had not yet told our children we were expecting. I had chosen a name for a girl, but not for a boy. And I would have no way of knowing if this child were he or she. No, we would not name this baby.

In the middle of that night, I woke with unusual cramps. When I rose to investigate, I found a tiny piece of tissue, smaller than the nail on my little finger, but unmistakably what the doctor told me to look for. I baptised conditionally and then very efficiently went to take care of this tissue, so tiny that I could hardly bring myself to think of it as a body. I put it in a rosary case, one that had a soft picture of the Madonna on it, and I put it in the freezer.

Still I did not grieve, but instead of sorrow, experienced something much worse. It was doubt. What is this to you, oh God? I asked. How can this tiny something-or-other matter in your eternal plan? And what is the point of answering our prayers for a new baby by sending us a piece of tissue resembling a human so little that I would have missed it had I not been carefully coached? I have never doubted that abortion was wrong, but in that moment, my pro-life convictions seemed silly; all that fuss over this little bit of tissue.

Name the baby? No, I wouldn't give a name to the contents of the rosary box in my freezer.

I went back to bed and rose the next morning to my usual routine. The miscarriage proceeded smoothly; no medical intervention was necessary. Winter prevented us from burying the rosary box immediately, so it stayed on in my freezer, getting moved further and further back behind the roasts, frozen vegetables and last summer's popsicles.

There were a few minor emotional after effects. I feared I would never have another baby, and in this fear, nothing was more consoling than the stories of so many friends who had miscarried and then gone on to have several more children. I also had trouble with prayer that can best be described as embarrassment. After begging God for this child, then thanking him lavishly when my prayers were answered, I didn't know what to say now. My doubts about the meaning of the miscarriage lingered. Why did this baby ever live at all?

One morning not long after the miscarriage, I was alone in the early hours, the time I find to read and pray. My husband and children still slept. I didn't pray; I thought about praying, wondering how to talk to God in the midst of these new discomforting doubts. Suddenly I saw a brilliant flash of light and heard a crash of music. Loud alleluias filled my house. I could see no one. Terrified, I ran to my bed, hiding underneath the blankets where my husband slept peacefully, unaware of the racket I endured.

Then, next to my ear, I thought I heard the unmistakable giggle of a baby. As the baby's chortling and the loud alleluias continued, I sensed a familiar touch. My soul felt lifted up and wrapped in God's powerful love. Fear left me. I'd had this experience before, a sense of God's presence that seems so certain it is physical.

How merciful our God is, to answer the questions of an impertinent doubter in such a profound and convincing manner. I don't believe God was trying to inform me that our lost baby is now a mascot for the heavenly choirs. But perhaps he wanted to remind me that my little one is his, was always his, as are all the little ones. Each human soul has eternal significance and has its part to play in God's plan of salvation, whether or not it appears important to our feeble senses.

The postscript to this story saw our family, on the first spring-like day of the year, at a Catholic cemetery. We brought our rosary box and a broken spade. Unfortunately, the ground was still too hard to turn, and try as we might, we simply could not make a hole in the ground big enough to accommodate even our tiny casket. We could do no more than crumble the topsoil. Frantic and upset, I finally let myself cry for the baby I would never know in this life, but my feelings of futility and meaninglessness were gone. In the end, I plucked a rose from a nearby grave, wrapped my tiny baby in its petals, and slipped the box underneath the bits of earth we had managed to dislodge.

We did not name the baby, but when it is my eldest daughter's turn to pick an intention for our rosary, she often says, 'for our rosepetal baby'. And when I think of the people God has sent into my life to reveal himself to me, this word, a name, comes to mind: *Rosepetal.*

Thirty

Karl Leisner, Priest in Dachau

by Elizabeth Haas

My brother, Karl, was born in Germany on February 28, 1915.
Our family, parents, two boys and three girls, lived quietly, as a
united and happy Catholic family. We explored the neighbouring
countryside on foot or on our bicycles. In the evening, we enjoyed
singing together. Our family, like many others in the years before
television, often sang, read and played games together.

At the age of thirteen, Karl joined the Catholic Youth Movement.
He liked the friends he made and their outdoor adventures. But
what he enjoyed most of all was the opportunity to learn a great
deal about God. Karl's heart and mind were opened to God,
helping him to accept the amazing adventure which became his
life . . . a life that included living in Dachau, a concentration camp
where innocent people, including priests, suffered and died at the
hands of Adolph Hitler's Nazi Party.

The first signs of the political troubles that lay ahead for Karl
came on July 3, 1933, when the principal of the high school ordered
him and his fellow classmates to sign a document in support of
Hitler and the Nazi party. It read, 'The undersigned students agree
that they will not work against the power or activities of the Nazi
Party'.

But by this time, Karl had already decided he wanted to become
a priest and in 1934 was sent to study for the priesthood in the city
of Münster, Germany. Almost immediately, the Bishop of Münster
recognised Karl's remarkable talents and told him that eventually

he would be needed to look after the young people of the diocese.

Fortunately, Karl kept a record of the day-to-day events in his life. This journal tells us about his personal thoughts, hopes, joys and fears. Our family remained enormously important to him, and at the age of 22 he wrote in his journal, 'I feel so at peace at home with my family, and how we pray for one another!' For a time Karl was torn by the question: did he have a genuine vocation to be a priest or was he really called to be a married man, bringing up a family of children just as our parents had done?

He put his problems to Our Lady, 'If I am to be a priest, let me know it and grant me the grace of overcoming myself, but if I am to become a bad priest, let me die first'. Eventually the conflict resolved, and Karl accepted wholeheartedly both his vocation to the priesthood and the responsibilities for youth which were to be put upon him by his bishop. 'My Lord', he wrote in his journal, 'with your blessing I will accept the heavy duty of leadership of the young; I dedicate all my energy to you, make me your instrument'.

My brother's fruitful work was indeed to lead young men and women, boys and girls around the world. But it was to be done through prayer, accomplished in loneliness and with much suffering.

The fact that Karl had accepted responsibility for the diocesan young people had not gone unnoticed by the Gestapo, Hitler's secret police. In 1936, suspicious of his activities, they opened a secret file on Karl. They noted such facts as that on New Year's Eve, 1937, he had spoken to some of his young people, telling them, 'We love Christ and will die for Christ'. The Gestapo wanted Germans to want to die for Hitler and the Nazi Party. They constantly watched Karl, checked his movements and read his mail.

On September 29, 1937, the Gestapo arrived at Karl's house at 7:15 am, made a thorough search of his rooms and confiscated his journals.

Greatly agitated, he took his bicycle and rode directly to Our Lady's Shrine at Kevelaer, knelt down in front of her statue and prayed to her Son, 'Thy will be done'.

There followed a period of apparent calm and Karl continued his studies for the priesthood. After a meditation on January 24, 1938, he wrote, 'O Christ, if you did not exist I should not want to be. You are. You live. Take me, for I am at your service.' By this time, Karl had a distinct sense of foreboding, of danger close at hand.

In 1939, the year of his ordination, Karl contracted tuberculosis in both lungs. The ordination was postponed because he was taken to a hospital in the Black Forest.

Within six months his health dramatically improved. On November 8, 1939, opponents of the Nazi Party attempted to bomb Hitler. The following morning, discussing the event with a fellow patient in his room in the hospital, Karl remarked that it was a pity Hitler hadn't been present at the time of the attack. For this remark, Karl was denounced to the authorities.

A patient accused Karl of being totally against Hitler, completely unimpressed by Hitler's views and that Karl believed that the survival of the Church in Germany would only be possible if the terrible enemy, Nazism, were to be overthrown.

Within hours, Karl was arrested. Two days later, my brother wrote secretly in his breviary, 'O my God, I thank you for the days of bondage and imprisonment. There is sense in everything: You only wish the very best for me.'

Granted permission, our mother visited Karl. They both accepted his imprisonment as God's will, and because of this, could cope in complete inner peace and charity. Externally, however, the situation soon deteriorated sharply. Nazi police moved Karl to the infamous Sachsenhausen prison near Berlin. Then Himmler, the leader of the SS, which included the secret police and storm troopers, ordered all priests to be confined in the same concentration camp, Dachau. Karl, as a sub-deacon, was also transferred to KZ Dachau.

In Dachau, as in all the KZ concentration camps, the main objective was to isolate, and ultimately to exterminate, all opposition to Hitler's Nazi Party. My brother, like all other prisoners in Dachau, ceased to be known by name and was given a mere number. Priests from 25 European countries crowded Barracks Numbers 26 to 30. A chapel was opened in Barrack No. 26 and here Karl found the Church in Chains.

Mass was said each morning at 5:00 am, just before dawn roll-call. Priests distributed Holy Communion and read the Divine Office. Religion study groups were organised. Jesus Christ himself was in Dachau, and the camp concealed an intense community spiritual life.

Although he experienced hours of deep depression, Karl gave no outward sign of the terrible inner trial he underwent, and his fellow prisoners remembered him for his cheerful disposition. He continued to long for his ordination to the priesthood, an event which in the circumstances of the time must have seemed to him highly improbable.

In September 1944, the situation changed. A new face appeared in Barrack No. 26, that of Bishop Gabriel Piguet of the diocese of Clermont-Ferrand in France. Secret messages were soon smuggled from Dachau to Karl's German superiors, Bishop von Galen of Münster and Cardinal Faulhaber of Munich, obtaining their official authorization for Karl's ordination by the French Bishop.

On December 17, 1944, weak and suffering from increasing illness, Karl was secretly ordained a priest of the Catholic Church. It was the only ordination of a priest to take place in a concentration camp of the Third Reich. 'It is not possible for me to express in words', he wrote less than two weeks later, 'my thanks for the manner in which God has granted me this unique favour, in answer to the prayers of his Blessed Mother. For the past 14 days I have been deeply affected.'

Weak and frail, Father Karl said his first Mass on the Feast of Saint Stephen, uniting himself with Christ in all the misery, all the humiliation, and all the suffering of Dachau. This first Mass of 'a priest in chains' was one of the happiest moments in the life of the appalling concentration camp. But for Karl, by now physically broken, his first Mass was also to be his last Mass.

On April 29, 1945, Americans liberated Dachau. Karl, too ill to stand, covered his face and wept. A local Catholic priest, Father Otto Pies, was allowed to enter the compound and five days later, on the Feast of Saint Monica, with the special permission of the authorities and the help of a somewhat unorthodox passport, Father Pies brought Father Karl out of the camp, carrying with him the Holy Eucharist.

From Dachau, Karl was taken immediately to a hospital in a forest near Munich, where he was received with great gentleness by the resident nuns and doctors. The hospital really seemed like paradise. 'Alone! In one's own room. What bliss!' he wrote in the diary. 'How infinitely good is God. He helps me always when the need is greatest. All he wanted was my total surrender. I received Holy Communion here early this morning and am so happy. Otto came to see me after Mass.'

The care of the good sisters began to take effect. 'Slowly the buried images of Dachau are beginning to loose their hold on me. I am a free man, hallelujah! I feel reborn! My human dignity is restored. Flowers on the table. The crucifix on the wall. A sister brings in a copy of Stephan Lochner's painting of Our Lady in Cologne Cathedral. I commend everything to her, my beloved Holy Mother! I pray to her, often, with tears in my eyes.'

Father Otto Pies observed my brother as he lay in the hospital. 'During the quiet days of his illness, Karl's inner spiritual growth, for which his long years of suffering had prepared him, proceeded apace, and I believe he developed an increasing understanding of the mystery of atonement.

'In Dachau, Karl had already offered his life to God as a sacrifice for the sake of young people. In spite of his increasing illness, his countenance and speech expressed quite clearly this newly-founded maturity and spiritual depth. He seldom thought about himself and rarely spoke about his own recent past. But everything that concerned the Church was of the utmost interest to him.'

On June 29, 1945, Karl had the enormous joy of being reunited with our dear parents with whom he had completely lost touch for six long years. 'Mother and Father are at my bedside, kissing and greeting them! Deeply moving. We are together again. *Deo gratias!*' But it was clear that the days in the concentration camp had taken their toll; Karl was weakening. He made his last diary entry on July 25, 1945. Mass had just been said by his bedside. 'Goodnight, eternal, holy God. Dear Blessed Mother. Good night all saints, all the loving, living and dead, near and far! Bless my enemies, O Lord!'

On August 9, 1945, my sister and I joined our parents at the hospital. The joy of seeing us all together allowed Karl to rally for a short time, and he carried on an animated conversation with us all. But then at noon, as we sat by his side, he once more fell back on his pillow and uttered his last words, 'I must suffer like the Saviour on the Cross'. Three days later he died. He was only 30 years old.

Although travel in Germany at that time was extremely difficult, it became possible for us, providentially, to take his body back to our home town. There, at Kleve, the inhabitants received him as a hero. The letters of condolences poured in. Karl's own bishop wrote to my parents, 'I believe, with confidence, that you have presented a saint to heaven'. The former chaplain of the Kleve Youth Movement also wrote, declaring that in his view a great son of the Church had just died, 'Karl is a model for us all; he is our intercessor'. Crowds soon began to visit his simple grave at Kleve, not only as individuals but also in groups, especially youth groups; memorial services and commemorations were held; streets, homes and a school were named after him.

In 1966, his body was exhumed and transferred to the Crypt of the martyrs in the local Cathedral. In 1972, the priests' Council of the Diocese of Münster requested that proceedings should be opened for his beatification. Four years later, having examined all the facts, Bishop Tenhumberg of Münster journeyed to Rome and proposed to the Holy Father, Pope Paul VI, that the cause of Father Karl Leisner should be opened, officially.

When receiving the request, His Holiness said, 'Karl Leisner, being purified by persecution and by personal suffering, being ordained priest in Dachau concentration camp in the face of death, sets an example worthy of imitation by more and more priests and believers'. On March 15, 1980, Pope John Paul II gave the final permission necessary for the opening of official proceedings for Father Karl's beatification. Later, when on his visits to Germany in 1980 and 1987, His Holiness made specific references to Karl. And again, in October 1988, when visiting the European Youth meeting in Strasbourg, the Holy Father quoted the priest from Dachau KZ, 'Christ is the mystery of European strength', and held him up as a model for young people. 'Poor Europe, return to your Lord Jesus Christ! Dear Lord, I plead with you, work through me as your instrument.' These words were written by Karl in June 1945, eight weeks before his death. Today, I know, more and more people are looking to my very dear brother as an intercessor for all young people, and as a powerful intercessor for Christian families throughout the world.

Thirty-One

I have Four Children, Not Three

by Jacqueline Engelhart

Four years ago today I sat numb, like a zombie, watching golf on TV. It was all I could do. That morning I had lost my baby, barely eight weeks into my pregnancy. My son, Christopher, was almost two at the time. Knowing fully the joy of having a baby, I was deeply in love with my little one. My pregnancy with Christopher had gone well; I never dreamed anything could go wrong, but in one short morning the whole thing was over. I had never felt so empty in my entire life.

But it is not over. I now have a very unique and beautiful relationship with my daughter. I have always had a very strong feeling that my baby was a girl. She has helped me so much. Emily, as we named her, is my own special 'tug' towards heaven. The thought that one day I will see her and hold her is a source of great comfort and consolation.

Emily is like my own personal little saint. My prayer is that all of my children will one day attain the joy of heaven, and now one of them is already there. I have asked her to intercede for me as I seek help and guidance in raising her older brother and her two other siblings who have since been born. In some ways our roles have been reversed; instead of me trying to teach and guide her in the path of the Lord, she is guiding me, 'tugging' me towards heaven.

Reaching the point where I could relate to Emily without crying or being confused or angry was a long and difficult process. There were many tears, time spent in prayer and a few sessions with a counsellor. I also had the help of a very loving and supportive husband. A year and a half after the miscarriage, I attended a beautiful service in my archdiocese for couples who had lost a child through miscarriage, stillbirth or abortion. This deeply moving service helped to bring a sense of closure to my grief. And of course the gift of time slowly but surely helped the healing process. I found one of my greatest sources of consolation in turning my child over to Mary. I asked her, the most perfect of all mothers, to be the mother of my daughter since I could not be with her. It brought me a tremendous sense of peace to know my daughter would be in Mary's protective and loving arms.

I still miss Emily very much; but I also thank God for Emily. Although I pray I may never have a miscarriage again, the whole experience taught me that ultimately we are not in control. God is. I find this fact both scary and comforting. It can be very disheartening to a person like me, always wanting to be in control, to have something like this happen. God is in control. I am not. The comforting aspect of this thought comes from believing in a God who loves me very much. He will take care of me. Five days after my miscarriage, I attended the Holy Thursday service and through it all one undeniable feeling came over me, God loves me. That's all that mattered. Everything would somehow be all right. I became totally convinced of it. It must have been the work of the Holy Spirit.

I sometimes remind myself I have four children, not three. I don't ever want to forget Emily. I have no picture or any other tangible proof that she ever existed, but she is as real as any person who ever lived. Thank you, Emily, for all you teach me and all you are for me. Thank you, Lord, for Emily. I anxiously await a joyful reunion in heaven.

Credits and Biographical Details

The pieces in this book originally appeared in the *Nazareth Journal* in the following editions and volumes:

Motherhood

Mariette Ulrich, 'My Master's Degree', *Nazareth* Vol. 6 No. 3, Fall 1996, pp. 26-30.

Catherine Fournier, 'My Pink T-Shirt', *Nazareth* Vol. 4 No. 2, Spring/Summer 1994, pp. 12-14.

Dianne Fuller, 'Miracles Along the Way', *Nazareth* Vol. 4 No. 2, Spring/Summer 1994, pp. 7-9.

Geraldine Hertz, 'At a Disadvantage', *Nazareth* Vol. 4 No. 3, Fall 1994, pp. 20-21.

Debbie Park, 'My Child is Handicapped', *Nazareth* Vol. 4 No. 2, Spring/Summer 1994, pp. 15-16.

Catherine Fournier, 'I am Third', *Nazareth* Vol. 5 No. 3, Fall 1995, pp. 23-25.

Fatherhood

James G. Anderson, 'The Pilgrimage', *Nazareth* Vol. 7 No. 2, Spring/Summer 1997, pp. 29-30.

Richard Nibogie, 'Brent', *Nazareth* Vol. 5 No. 2, Spring/Summer 1995, pp. 8-10.

Don Ellis, 'Our Son's Brush with Death', *Nazareth* Vol. 7 No. 3, Fall 1997, pp. 8-9.

Michael O'Brien, 'Disaster, Rage and Repentance', *Nazareth* Vol. 5 No. 1, Lent 1995, pp. 10-15.

Robert Otrembiak, 'Mary Helen', *Nazareth* Vol. 5 No. 3, Fall 1995, pp. 14-15.

Petroc Willey, 'Forgiveness, Stars, and Saint God', *Nazareth* Vol. 5 No. 4, Advent 1995, pp. 16-18.

Marriage

Maria Delft, 'I Buried Jesus, Mum', *Nazareth* Vol. 3 No. 3, Advent 1993, pp. 17-20.

Astrid Nordholt, 'Not Your Will, But Mine', *Nazareth* Vol. 4 No. 3, Fall 1994, pp. 16-19.

Catherine Fournier, 'A Day in a Catholic Marriage', *Nazareth* Vol. 5 No. 1, Lent 1995, pp. 16-20.

Joan Barrow, 'Snow and Roses', *Nazareth* Vol. 3 No. 3, Advent 1993, pp. 10-12.

Catherine Fournier, 'I Will if I Have To, But Please Don't Ask Me', *Nazareth* Vol. 7 No. 1, Lent 1997, pp. 41-43.

Family Life

Catherine Fournier, 'Quietly Running Taps', *Nazareth* Vol. 4 No. 3, Fall 1994, pp. 8-10.

Geraldine Hertz, 'The House That Love Built', *Nazareth* Vol. 5 No. 1, Lent 1995, pp. 6-9.

Astrid Nordholt, 'Jesus was an Only Child', *Nazareth* Vol. 7 No. 2, Spring/Summer 1997, pp. 31-33.

Catherine Fournier, 'Sleeping in the Barn on Christmas Eve', *Nazareth* Vol. 3 No. 3, Advent 1993, pp. 21-24.

Michael D. O'Brien, 'Catechesis and Evangelisation', in two parts, *Nazareth* Vol. 7 No. 2, Spring/Summer 1997, pp. 12-15 and *Nazareth* Vol. 7 No. 3, Fall 1997, pp. 24-27.

Autumn Years

Francis Phillips, 'Making Room at the Inn', *Nazareth* Vol. 3 No. 3, Advent 1993, pp. 34-35.

Geraldine Hertz, 'Father and Father-in-Law', *Nazareth* Vol. 5 No. 2, Spring/Summer 1995, pp. 11-14.

Paul Lissandrello, 'Still Bearing Fruit', *Nazareth* Vol. 7 No. 3, Fall 1997, pp. 21-23.

Ed Billet, 'The Miraculous Medal and Me', *Nazareth* Vol. 4 No. 2, Spring/Summer 1994, pp. 17-20.

Eternal Life

Ellie Hrkach, 'Five Little Souls in Heaven', *Nazareth* Vol. 5 No. 2, Spring/Summer 1995, pp. 31-33.

Abigail Hearth, 'New Life', *Nazareth* Vol. 7 No. 3, Fall 1997, pp. 12-13.

Mariea Hall, 'Rosepetal', *Nazareth* Vol. 5 No. 1, Lent 1995, pp. 25-26.

Elizabeth Haas, 'Karl Leisner, Priest in Dachau', *Nazareth* Vol. 4 No. 2, Spring/Summer 1994, pp. 42-44.

Jacqueline B. Engelhart, 'I have Four Children Not Three', *Nazareth* Vol. 7 No. 2, Spring/Summer 1997, pp. 38-39.

Biographical details:

Michael O'Brien, former editor of the *Nazareth Journal*, is an internationally known painter, novelist and essayist, endeavouring to further the renewal and revitalisation of Christian culture. He is the author of the *Children of the Last Days* series, and has recently published *Island of the World*, a tale of the crucifixion and resurrection of a soul set in the twentieth century Balkans. The Nazareth Family Apostolate ended its retreat ministry in 1992, yet the work it had begun continued in similar new apostolates to the family throughout the world. *Nazareth Journal* published its final issue in 1998.

Sr Crucis Beards, FMDM, has spent most of her working life in Zambia, Southern Africa, working in the health ministry, initially as a nurse/midwife teacher and then latterly in an HIV/AIDS hospice, which she jointly founded with local Zambian laity. Sister Crucis obtained an MA in Higher Education from the University of Surrey in 1996 and then later an MA from Maryvale Institute. Currently, Sister Crucis is Research Assistant at The Maryvale Institute, Centre for Marriage and Family, where she hopes to develop a Theology of the Body programme for use in Africa.

Anna Schafer joined the faculty of The Maryvale Institute in 2006, where she presently has responsibility for publications and works closely with the BA in Applied Theology programme. She is a graduate of Franciscan University of Steubenville, Ohio, USA, where she studied Catholic Theology, Humanities and Catholic Culture. Born and raised on a dairy farm in northwestern Minnesota, USA, she has particular interest in Catholic culture and Catholic rural life.